How Not To Dad

A mostly humorous memoir of the
struggles of fatherhood

Luke Whaley

This book is dedicated to my father, Keith Whaley, for providing the benchmark for what a dad should be. Thanks for setting the bar so high, pop!

INTRODUCTION

Welcome to my world, a world of boogers, crying, aging, farts, vomit, absent-mindedness, hugs, shame, and laughter. In these pages I document my first five years of fatherhood, with a healthy dose of emphasis on the situational challenges that arise with raising young kids. Make no mistake, if you came here to learn something useful about parenting you're most likely not going to find it. You will, however, discover a good sampling of what not to do, and hopefully have a few laughs while doing it. This book is part memoir, part anti-instruction manual, and part treatise on the common male parenting experience. If you've ever felt like you don't know what in the hell you're doing raising your kids on a daily basis, read this, nod to yourself, and bask in the understanding that there's at least one more clueless dad out there. Namely, me.

And one more thing: snap buttons suck.

How Not To Dad

PROLOGUE

A Tale of Two Kiddies

<u>1</u>

I entered the realm of dadhood in two very different ways. Our first kid, Logan, is my stepson and I met him when he was roughly ten months old. His mother and I started dating just after his first birthday.

One of my earliest memories of feeling the dad experience (more to the point, the *new* dad experience) was at a McDonald's in our small town in Alabama. Like many one-year-olds, one of Logan's strongest personality traits was that he absolutely could not handle being still for anything more than four seconds, so being strapped into a high chair was not very high on his list of things he liked to do. There was another thing that occupied a bullet point at the lower end of that list: eating. To this day, seven years later, the boy damn near refuses to eat anything.

We chose our table that night at McDonald's and as soon as Logan was seated in his high chair he started getting fussy. After about five minutes the whines became more frantic. Nikki and I had known each other for several months, but had not been dating for more than a couple of weeks at this time. I have always loved kids, but I was a mid-thirties guy who lived alone and was used to dining in relative silence. Plus, I had the old streak of my own dad in me, and my dad had always been adamant about how we behaved in public. He also knew how to put the fear of God in you with a simple look, a skill I had yet to develop at the time.

Side note: since then my dad look has improved by leaps and bounds. Seems my fifteen minutes of practice each day in front of a mirror has paid off.
Just kidding.
Sort of.

Logan began screaming and crying. He wouldn't eat.

Being that single guy for so long, I knew what others in the restaurant were thinking because I'd thought it myself whenever I'd see or hear an unruly child in public. I could almost hear the words:

Get your kid under control, will you?
Somebody needs to teach that kid to behave.
Take him outside if he's going to act like that.
Swat his ass a few times. that'll get him to stop.

It's the type of thing everyone who has not been a parent before has thought. I always assumed I'd operate under those same thought processes when I became a parent, yet here I was, listening to a child scream because he didn't want to eat his food, and I had no idea what to do about it.

You want to see how naive I was? I leaned in to face this little one-year-old, tried on the scary dad face, and authoritatively stated: "Stop it right now."

Any guesses on how much impact that had? Anyone? You in the back? That's right. None. No effect, except to make him start a new round of wailing while his mother looked at me like I had just assaulted the child.

We'd only been dating a couple of weeks, and later she told me that she wasn't quite ready at the time for anyone else to try and discipline her kid. She'd had a year's worth of parenting under her belt, and had already come to the understanding that I had not yet grasped. Kids are going to act up. They're going to scream and make a scene and the best thing you can do in the moment is try to diffuse the situation.

That was one of the first lessons I learned about parenting, and it was a huge one for me. It took me months to acclimate to it, because I don't particularly like attention so getting negative attention from random people during a child's outburst didn't sit too well with me.

Logan and I became best buds in the following weeks, and though it took three years of dating for me to propose to his mom (my commitment issues are for a whole other book, so we won't delve into that), I realized early on that this little guy was an essential part of my life. I loved him as much as I loved his mom, and my life wouldn't be complete without him in it. Kids have this sneaky way of becoming your whole life, and it doesn't take them long to do it.

Crafty little buggers, they are.

<u>2</u>

My second introduction to dadhood began in a darkened room on a fuzzy monitor screen. I wrote the following a few days afterward.

<u>The Ultrasound</u>

When the image appeared I didn't know what to think or where to look. A mass of white noise shifted and contracted on the screen. No sounds were heard. No shapes I could identify. Then, a moment later, a black hole opened in the center of the screen and inside it, a little mass hung suspended. It didn't move. Having never been present for an ultrasound I had no idea if that was normal or not.

We had come to Nikki's doctor a few days earlier than scheduled because Nikki had gotten a stomach bug and, while experiencing all the joys that only a stomach virus can bring you, noticed a possible complication. She grew nervous, as did I, and she called the doc to see if we could push the appointment up a few days.

So there we were in the ultrasound room. It was dark. Had a bit of a dinner-at-a-fine-restaurant type mood lighting going. My wife was lying on the examination table. I was looking at what could have been an old television on an unused station, if not for the blackness in the middle and the way the particles move on the screen and, of course, the spot in the center. The unmoving spot. I held my breath, waiting for the nurse to frown or scrunch up one corner of her mouth in pity at the news she was about to deliver. I think Nikki and I were both bracing for that.

"There's the heartbeat." She said instead.

In the center of that mass, a tiny translucent ball swelled and contracted fitfully. The nurse then turned on the sound, and a steady *wah-wah-wah-wah* hit my ears and instantly drew tears from my eyes. My mouth hung open, I didn't blink, I just watched the little blob with its heart beating over and over again. I didn't want it to stop.

"Everything looks good." The nurse said.

You're damn right it does, I thought. *That's my baby!*

(Okay I didn't actually think that last part until just now but basically, yeah, that's the sentiment I've got.)

A few months after that moment, our baby arrived. I kept notes throughout the day of the birth of our daughter. I didn't bother with great punctuation or grammar. I left this entry unaltered, as I had typed it on my phone that day.

The Birth of Abby Kate

(I typed the below text the day that Abby was born, on my phone at various points throughout the day…)

It is a surreal experience to say the least to see your child being born. For months we'd gone to appointments and felt the baby move inside Nikki's belly. We'd watched a ghosted image of her on the ultrasound screen. I knew she was there, a physical being squirming with life behind a thin wall of flesh. It was hard, though, to imagine the real person that she was. I knew my child was alive and deserving of everything I could possibly give her, yet it was hard not to think of her as a distant thing. A beloved relative from a distant land who was planning to visit. A situation that was GOING to happen, but since we didn't know when it would happen it always felt like a hypothetical, especially since we'd been back and forth with the staff at OBGYN South on when Nikki was going to be induced.

At any rate, this was no longer a hypothetical situation. This was real. I had no choice but to prepare for an entirely new life and to hopefully give the best parts of me to this child, who was soon to take her first breaths in this world.

Nikki pushed three times, and Abby's head edged closer to freedom. Once the third push was done, the doctor told her to breathe. Nikki laid back on the bed and waited until the next set of contractions came, which seemed like only a minute or so.

Once it hit her again she leaned forward and pushed. It was harder the second time.

"I need you to push harder," the doctor said.

"I can't!" Nikki said.

"You can do it you're doing great." He answered.

"You're doing awesome!" I said. "She's right there. She's almost here!"

She pushed three times. Abby's head was crowning, a white bowl with black wriggles of hair streaking it. The contractions hit again and Nikki bared down. She grasped the bed rails. I held her leg, and nurse Julie held the other.

Nikki let out a grunt/growl that lasted through the push as her body forced the little one's head through. Once the top of the baby's head exited, Dr. Aldred told her to give one more push and the shoulders were free too. Our baby was in the doctor's hands.

I don't know what happened immediately after that. I know they used one of those snot sucker things to remove any liquid from Abby's mouth and nose. I know I heard the high-pitched, scraping cry of a little girl who was just learning how to use that voice. I will never forget that cry.

But why I can't remember all the specifics of the few minutes directly following the birth was that I was an emotional wreck. The minute her head fully exited the birth canal, tears broke through as if a dam had burst inside of me. I couldn't see anything but blurs. I didn't move. I stood there at the bed rail and cried like I hadn't cried in years. I just couldn't believe that I was looking at this new life, a life I helped create. A life for which I was responsible. All of our preparation and all the anticipation had led to this single moment for me, the crescendo of an eight week journey. If hearing my daughter's heartbeat for the first time at the ultrasound was life-changing, this was almost a religious experience. Never had I felt so connected not only to the baby but to my wife and son as well.

This solidified the fourth member of our family. We would never be the same.

They laid Abby down on Nikki's chest once they'd done the preliminary check on her. I took a few pics, and one of the nurses took one of the three of us with my camera. By that time I had mostly dried up the tears. After the pic I sort of snapped out of it and followed as they took the baby to a little bed underneath a heat lamp to clean her off.
I took several pictures there while the doctor helped Nikki finish the delivery process. In my state of wonder I had forgotten that Nikki still had to "deliver" the placenta, and I assume the doctor checked for any injuries or tearing. Nikki was lucky. Not much medical attention was needed, she'd just be sore for a while.
After Abby was sufficiently cleaned and her footprint was scanned (they apparently no longer do the print with ink) I went into the waiting room, where our parents had been joined by my brother Kevin. I hugged my dad and told everyone the news. Baby was born, both she and her mother were doing fine. Nikki wanted Logan to be the first to see her, so I brought him back with me and he walked into the room with a big smile on his face. I pointed to Abby. He tentatively stepped towards the little bed with the heating lamp hanging over it, and greeted his baby sister.

These two kids, Logan and Abby, have changed my life so much that there is no possible way I could go back to living as I had before. They are everything to my wife and I. Still, just because they mean so much doesn't mean I don't screw up royally on a regular basis while raising them.

What follows is a record of such screw ups.

CHAPTER 1

THE WALMART FIASCO OFFICIAL REPORT

<u>Travelling From/To</u>: Home in Hanceville, AL / Wal-Mart in Cullman, AL (Approx. 6miles)

<u>Mission Intent</u>: Spend time with my baby daughter, do some light shopping, maybe visit a park and walk with the stroller, return home with a nice little memory of a perfect father-daughter day.

<u>Result</u>: Promising beginning; eventual chaos

<u>Grade</u>: F

Details

My wife was out of town. My stepson was at his dad's. I was alone with a six month old. This was exciting to me, as I love one-on-one time with my kids. I get Abby fed, get her dressed in her *Batgirl* onesie, and even find matching purple pants in the labyrinth that is her dresser drawers. I'm wearing dad-approved navy blue cargo shorts, a *Leprechaun* movie t-shirt (I'm a horror movie fanatic) and flip flops. So yeah, we look cool.

The first task once we were properly attired was to prepare the diaper bag. To all who are unfamiliar, the diaper bag is a literal bottomless pit of baby products that you'll need on any quest into civilization. Things to remember: diapers, wipes, formula, bottles, water, extra clothes, bibs, spit up towels, pacifiers, teething toys, regular toys, sunscreen, blanket, first aid kit, survival knife, rope, harness, helmet, map, compass, lip balm, flashlights, batteries, matches, extra day's supply of food, water treatment system, signaling mirror, walking stick, and a full set of metric deep-well sockets and wrenches. And you damn well better not forget one thing on this list, or your baby will definitely remind you.

So I gather all the components. I fix up a little three compartment canister that holds enough formula for three bottles. I set it aside and prepare the bottles with warm water. I do a quick check to make sure there are diapers, extra clothes, wipes, a towel, and all the other stuff, then I zip up the bag and get Abby in her car seat. I bump her head against the seat handle as I ease her in. This triggers an eruption of tears and I do all I can to comfort her. Eventually I gave her one of her teething toys and she lost interest in crying so I buckled her in.

Slinging the diaper bag over one arm (my wife is tiny, and I couldn't wrangle my other arm through the backpack strap), I carry the bag out to the car. I come back in, grab my cup of coffee, pick up the car seat, and stand at the door for several seconds like a Neanderthal as my mind works out how I'm going to open the door while holding both the car seat and a cup of hot coffee. The answer is NOT, I finally realize, to hold the car seat and coffee in the same hand while opening the door with the other. Eventually my mind works through this problem and I proceed, pausing again on the other side of the door to figure out how the hell I'm going to close it.

We make it into the car and begin our day. Abby falls asleep as I drive. I go through Jack's drive thru and grab some breakfast that I eat in Wal-Mart's parking lot once we arrive, while Abby naps.

She wakes up when I get her out. I'm pretty clever, I realize, because I decide to park beside the cart return station. This way I can get her out and place the car seat in a shopping cart immediately, and don't have to lug the car seat all the way into the store.

I've got this shit figured out, y'all. This trip's gonna be a breeze.

Abby is all smiles as we make our way through the front doors. I go to the electronics section first and pick out a couple of movies. Then I head to the men's clothes and choose a few things. I stop by the arts and crafts section and get some canvases (canvi…?). So far, so good. Abby grunts and wriggles a couple of times here and there, but I dismiss it as mild discomfort. She is content as always. I even go to the baby section and look at the toys.

And here is where it all begins to unravel.

Abby starts to fuss. I think to myself, *she's getting tired of the car seat. Get her out of the car seat and hold her. You'll have a free hand to push the cart. What could go wrong?*

One thing that could go wrong would consist of me banging her head against the car seat handle as I get her out. Again. Causing - again - an eruption of crying that I have to try and soothe away while tending to the buggy with my other hand. So I try the usual method, I begin to walk and lightly bounce her in my arm. Only now I'm wielding a Wal-Mart shopping cart with one hand, trying to steer it between racks of baby clothes while calmly talking to my daughter the way I do when I want her to go to sleep.

I knew I was really in trouble when her elephant teething toy didn't calm her down. Normally you can hand her that and it goes straight to her mouth, and she's immediately absorbed with chewing on it. Instead she continued to cry and I awkwardly shuffled through the aisles holding a sobbing baby in one arm and pushing the shopping cart with the other.

Can't put her back in the car seat now. It'll just piss her off more.

I shamble down the large aisle in the rear of the store. Finally Abby begins calming down. Her teething toy is beginning to work its magic, and inwardly I sigh in relief.

Until I realize I can't reach my wallet to pay for the stuff in the cart.

It's in my back pocket, on the same side where I'm holding Abby. Neanderthal Luke reemerges, standing in the children's clothes section with a baby in one arm and a shopping cart full of crap at my side, probably looking like I'm trying to figure out how to add one plus one.

Hey idiot, let go of the shopping cart and switch the baby to the other side so you can reach it, my brain says after it apparently reboots. With a clumsy, not-so-swift motion that tried to be a swift motion, I shifted the baby to the other arm and grab my wallet.

In order to extract a debit card you need two hands. One hand to hold the wallet, and the other hand to pull the card from it. I manage to get my wallet into the hand that is holding the baby, and Abby and I fight for a moment over who gets the card once I pull it out. She fusses a little, but finds her teething toy again and all is calm. I shove the card in my pocket and head for the front of the store.

I make it to the registers. No way in hell am I going to attempt a self checkout like this, so I find a lane and wait my turn.

Abby does not have the same problem my son Logan had at this age. Logan hated standing still. We always dreaded getting to the checkout lines because the minute we stopped he started pitching a fit. Abby, on the other hand, sits on my arm and gnaws on her toy elephant, and just looks at everything. She's back to her old self, content and happy.

There's a light at the end of the tunnel. I see it. We're gonna make it, little sis. The day is still ours.

We check out. The lady at the register and the elderly lady behind me make a fuss over how cute and little Abby is. They talk to her and she looks at them and even half-ass waves at them as we walk away.

Feeling the weight lifting further off my shoulders by the second, I proudly carry my daughter into the parking lot like a mighty warrior returning from battle. Yes, I've lost a few men, we're both wounded and beaten down, and she's got a head injury, but we survived. We fought the good fight and have lived to see another day.

Neanderthal Luke makes a final appearance once I stop the buggy at the trunk of my car. With but a moment's hesitation, I sweep the dumbass side of myself away, grab the fob from my keychain, and push the button that pops the trunk. I sling the bags in the trunk with my free hand. I grab the car seat (much lighter when it's empty) and set it on the base that's strapped into the back seat, return the buggy, and stand there with my baby in my arm, feeling successful.

Triumphant even.

Hell, let's get her fed before we do anything else, I think. *We've got a few hours worth of water and formula and spare diapers. Let's brush off the problems we've had and make a day of it.*

I slide the driver's seat as far back as it can go, and then ease into the car with the baby. Abby slaps at the steering wheel as I reach for her diaper bag so I can make her a bottle. We're having fun now! I unzip the bag and open it up, pull the bottle out (already filled with water because I'm a genius), and then reach in for my canister of pre-made formula that I so precisely measured and filled for three separate bottles, and-

Hmmm. Don't see it.

Nah, it's there. I remember packing it. It's probably underneath the spare clothes. I shuffle things around a bit in search of the little container.

Confusion leads to uncertainty.

Uncertainty leads to panic.

Panic eventually leads to realization.

I thought back: I had measured all the scoops of formula, snapped the lid on, and then set it on the kitchen island so I could make the bottles, then I put the bottles in the bag, checked for diapers, wipes, clothes, and burp cloths.

Here's the kicker: *Nowhere in that list of activities did I place the damn formula in the diaper bag.* So now I'm sitting with a time bomb in my lap. A time bomb that might speed up if I put her back in her car seat. And I do indeed have to put her back in the car seat, right? Yes, I have to remind myself half jokingly. (Okay, okay, I know you can't drive through town with an infant in your lap. Still, there's that voice that sneaks in, whispers shit like *you're a good driver, don't worry the cops'll never see her. Just drive.* I hate that guy.)

This is where my daughter comes in clutch, and saves the day. I had resigned myself to facing a car ride home to the tune of my daughter's rageful cries. Instead she calmly looked at me as I placed her in her car seat and allowed me to buckle her in. We rode home. I still held a tiny ray of hope that I would be up for going back to town after we'd been home for a while and Abby had gotten a nap, but I think I knew our trip was done. Still, my daughter is amazing. She goes with the flow more than any child I have ever seen. She proved that by remaining calm on the ride home, though she must have started getting hungry. I don't know if I thanked her out loud for not losing her shit, but I did in my mind for sure. And I thank her now.

<u>Moral of the story</u>: Dudes, check your diaper bag. Double check your diaper bag. Triple check your diaper bag. At

minimum food, diapers, wipes, and extra clothing absolutely must be with you at all times.

Or you will be destroyed.

CHAPTER 2

Speed Bag

There are two problems I have with furniture at my home right now. Two things that have come together to cause more pain than any man should have to endure.

#1: We bought a new bed two years ago. Not just any new bed, mind you. A fancy new bed. This is the kind of bed that comes with a freakin' remote, and can lift your head or your feet to get you in the most comfortable position possible (turns out the most comfortable position possible, by the way, is laying flat). The thing about a bed like this is that all the mechanics have to be mounted underneath the bed, and that means the bed itself is raised from the floor a foot or so to account for all that excess technology.

Now, the average box spring is about nine inches thick. The average mattress is maybe twelve inches thick. Add the foot of height for the mechanical frame, and that gets you to about 2'-9" from the floor to the top of your bed's mattress. Let's hold that dimension in the back of our minds as we proceed.

#2: My wife bought our six-month-old daughter a bouncy seat. It's basically big plastic ring that is covered in toys, and the ring is attached by elastic bands to three posts that connect to the base of this beast. In the middle of the ring is a seat where the baby sits. You have to feed her little feet into the appropriate holes so her legs hang below the ring.

For an average baby this puts their feet on the floor beneath them. Our daughter is small, so she just sort of dangled there when we first attempted to set her in it. To fix this my wife got one of the fifty throw pillows that came with our couch and put it underneath Abby's feet as extra support.

Abby loves it. She pushes off the pillow below her and bounces up and down over and over again, causing all the little rattle toys to clatter with each bounce as if it were the Godzilla of maracas (side note: I was today years old when I realized you don't spell maraca like the west African country Morocco). She's becoming more and more mobile. Her little legs are getting a daily workout, building strength that will one day help her to take her first steps.

Okay. Now we've established the two objects that have caused me such pain. If you don't see the connection yet, give me one more minute.

A possible side effect of Abby's love for this bouncy seat is her desire to pretend she's in it when she's not. Sitting up or laying down, she occasionally goes into kicking fits when she's excited.

I realize today that my daughter's been training her legs for weeks on that damned bouncy seat, building muscle tone, getting leaner and more powerful, and I can only imagine a *Rocky* style montage scene of her training for the day she fights her arch nemesis using her legs instead of her fists as her weapons of destruction. Had I known who (or, rather, *what)* her arch nemesis might be, I might have trained too. Maybe learned some dodging techniques.

We have a changing station that sits on Abby's dresser, covered in the mountains of clothes we've bought or been given as hand-me-downs. We never use it. It's much easier, we've found, to lay Abby on our nice expensive bed and change her there. Not long ago I laid her down, right at that 2'-9" bed height you'll remember from earlier, and began changing her diaper. I'm 5'-8"-ish tall, which would put my mid-section at just under the 3'-0" mark. Say, maybe 2'-9".

I place her gently on the bed, and I stand against the bed's edge. I have a clean diaper in hand. Half leaning on the bed facing my daughter, I open the clean diaper like I always do and prepare for a swift change, and my view of Abby is blocked by said diaper. I am less than a foot away from her. At this point, unbeknownst to me, my daughter has decided to do her leg exercises. And here, virtually resting atop the edge of the bed, is her speed bag.

She kicks.

I jolt as her feet batter my man bag like Liu Kang from *Mortal Kombat* doing his bicycle kick.

I almost buckle and fall directly onto her. Luckily, I catch myself. My daughter looks up at me as if I were nothing more interesting than a potato. She has no idea she single-handedly prevented herself from ever having more siblings.

I stand up.

Wipe the tears from my eyes.

Wait for my nuts to come out of my stomach.

After that I finish changing my daughter, this time giving her pumped up legs the respect they deserve.

<u>Moral of the story</u>: Protect your coconuts, boys. Just because they don't know what they're doing doesn't mean babies won't knock your nuggets up into your throat if your attention lags for even a second.

CHAPTER 3

Poop

Little boy humor alert: We're sitting at Burger King, where Logan and I always go for breakfast when we're alone, and Logan says: "My food tasted like hash brown poop." That drew a laughing "What?!" From me, which only served to spur him on.

"Mine tasted like cricket poop."

(I laugh)

"Mine tasted like pee poop."

(I laugh)

"Mine tasted like octopus poop."

(I laugh)

Then the game goes to both of us alternating the saying, coming up with different silly words and adding poop to it.

Notables:

"Mine tasted like King Kong poop"   (then he says "King Kong's poop would look like a big potato.")

"Mine tasted like truck poop."

"Mine tasted like human poop."

"Mine tasted like my poop." I laugh and ask what again, and try to shush Logan when he says with a smile "I eat my own poop."

"Mine tasted like bird poop."

There was worm poop and light bulb poop and pancake poop. Deep conversations on a Saturday morning.

CHAPTER 4

Night Terrors

I spent a ton of time in haunted houses in my twenties and early thirties. It was what my friends and I did. Around Halloween time, several local attractions would pop up in our area and we'd travel sometimes out of state to visit the most notorious of them. We even visited real haunted locations, like Waverly Hills Sanatorium in Louisville. I think we all loved that constant buzz of adrenaline, that anticipation of what's going to happen next.

Is a chainsaw-wielding clown going to pop out of the corner and chase me through the trail?

Is that mannequin *really* a mannequin?

What's tickling my leg?

Do you hear that sound?

Who's screaming?

When things get quiet is when the real terror begins. That's when someone - or some *thing* - is gearing up to try and scare at least a moderate-sized squirt of piss out of you. That's when you need to be on your toes, you know?

Fast-forward to today. On some nights, I live in a haunted house. The haunts in my home are unhappy children sent to bed thirsty, or babies mad that they can't sleep in bed with their mommy.

One night last week my wife and I put our son to bed, and then carried our daughter to her little playpen bed in our room. After Abby fell asleep, my wife and I laid down and watched a couple of episodes of *The Office* until we fell asleep.

The first phantom appeared before midnight. A little boy, about five years old. It touched my shoulder and I rolled over to face it while half asleep and coming out of a dream.

"Can I have a cup of water?" The ghost whispered.

I motioned towards a bottle of water on my night stand. "Take it," I murmured. The thought of this phantom returning to his room and peeing the bed didn't occur to me. I just wanted my sleep back. The ghost soon vanished.

Ten minutes later the second ghost wailed into the night from the foot of my bed. I jerked out of sleep, my eyes open wide. The sound dissipated, and I started to think I had imagined it when a rustling came from the same place.

Then another moan.

I laid perfectly still. I prayed this little ghost wouldn't hear me and wake up screaming.

After several minutes of lying there stiff as a corpse I finally began to doze again. The movement at the foot of the bed ceased. I sank into sleep, feeling its warm arms envelope me as I drifted further and further from consciousness.

"Mommy!" Something called from the other room.

My eyelids twitched open. *What time is it?*

"Mommy!"

My stomach shriveled. Goosebumps sprouted on my arms. Some part of me hearkened back to those childhood fears from watching too many horror movies. There's just something really unsettling about hearing voices shouting from somewhere in a dark house in the middle of the night.

Even if it *is* your son.

"MOMMY!"

I look at my wife, who is shifting in our bed, half asleep.

I couldn't tell if I was fully awake or dreaming the sound. The eerie sensation lingered. My fear, though, was not of a supernatural entity waiting to harvest my soul the minute I stepped off the bed to go investigate. My fear was a sick child. Not only do you not want your kid to be in pain, you also don't want to be scrubbing hurl out of their bedroom carpet at 2:00 a.m. on a weeknight.

"MOMMY!"

My wife's eyes are half open.

"What is it Logan?" She calls out.

We've got to be careful. The other little ghost has fallen asleep no more than six feet away. We don't need a double haunting.

"Come in here, Logan." I call, hoping to somehow trick the properties of sound into allowing a shout that is also a whisper. The delicate balance holds. My daughter remains asleep.

A door opens somewhere.

Footsteps thump across the hall.

Our bedroom door swings open, spilling light from the hallway across our bed. A figure stands there. "My tooth hurts." He says.

Nikki and I look at each other, then back at Logan.

"Um, which one hurts? The wiggly one?" Nikki asks.

"Uh-huh," he whines. I can tell by his posture that he's half asleep. His shoulders are slumped, and his head is hanging at an angle like he's trying to hold it up but doesn't have enough energy. I think it hits both Nikki and I at the same moment that he's sleepwalking. He'd gone to the dentist that day and had gotten a good report. His tooth shouldn't be hurting. (I never verified if he was dreaming about the dentist, but I did ask him the next day if his tooth still hurt. "Nope." he said.)

"Go back to bed and get to sleep, baby." Nikki tells him. "It'll feel better in the morning."

Logan shuffles off. We hear his door close.

While Nikki fell back asleep, I laid on my back staring at the ceiling. The barrage of waking jolts kept me on edge. I couldn't help but lay there anticipating the next jump scare. I was like a kid trying to wait out a storm, knowing that next thunderclap is coming but not knowing when.

An hour later I finally made it to sleepytown. The next time I awoke it was to the wail of an alarm clock. I roll out of bed, the events of last night now a fading memory. My body sure as hell remembers, though. I've become a zombie for the day, shambling through the hallways and cubicles at my workplace in voracious search not for brains but for coffee. That sweet, delicious potion that has the ability to rouse the dead and hold the ghosts of last night at bay.

At least until tonight.

<u>Moral of the Story</u>: Sleep all you can. Sleep is good. Sleep is life. Sleep. Sleep. Sleepysleepsleep.... sleep. zzzz... zzzzzzzz....

CHAPTER 5

Koumpounophobia

To begin this next chapter, what I'd like to do is ship a flux capacitor laden Delorean to the corner of Gitschiner street and Linden street in Berlin, Germany, set the displays to March 5, 1885, back that sumbitch up about a quarter of a meile (that's mile to us English speaking folk), aim it at the German Patent Office, and gun it. If there is any true sense of fate or destiny in this crazy universe, and a kneifen (pinch) or two of luck, I'd meet the sidewalk to that building at the exact moment that a gentleman named Heribert Bauer is strolling his happy arsch into the patent office, probably carrying an envelope with some documents and a little prototype metal object a bit smaller than a dime stuffed into it. Hopefully the time machine would materialize just close enough to Mr. Bauer so that the DMC logo on the grill would rustle his pant leg as it screamed to a stop an inch from his knees.

In the nice version this would happen, and Bauer would fling the envelope into the air and scamper away unharmed. I'd pick the envelope up, throw it in a trashcan somewhere, then start trying to figure out how I'd get back home since you can't get plutonium in Berlin in 1885. It's not available at every corner store yet.

In the not so nice version, the Delorean doesn't stop inches from the knees, if you know what I mean. Either way, the envelope and its contents must be destroyed, for the happiness of dads everywhere.

What's in the envelope, you ask? What little metal object can cause such rage as to inspire me to want to bend space-time itself, risking all of existence in order to stop this object from being invented altogether?

The snap button. The snap button is what's in the envelope. What Mr. Bauer (or the man who perfected the design almost twenty years later, or the thousands of textile workers and designers who slap these little metal bastards all over baby clothes) didn't take into account was that you can't really snap thirty-eight buttons together from ankles to nipples of a wriggling baby who's pissed off because she has to wear clothes.

The common baby has two legs. For some reason, someone once decided it would be a good idea to put a row of buttons up both legs that met in the middle, so you can unsnap all of these buttons quickly for easy access to the diaper. It works, too! Getting the onesie undone is pretty easy when dealing with buttons.

Getting the onesie back on, though, is like trying to do a jigsaw puzzle while riding a unicycle during an earthquake. My daughter is a calm baby, but even calm babies have pretty short fuses when you're trying to snap the "male" side of the button to the "female" side only to find after three or four buttons that the "male" side is a cheating bastard and is sticking his appendage in the wrong partner. So you unsnap, re-snap, do the same with the other leg, and when you get to the joint where the legs meet the hips you find two "female" side buttons staring at each other. Now you've got to rework the buttons and try to figure out how they became lesbians somewhere along the way.

Now try doing all that while your pissed off baby is screaming and kicking at your face.

<u>Moral of the Story:</u> If your wife takes you shopping for baby clothes and gets all excited about an outfit for your daughter and asks your opinion, you only need to be looking for one thing: how many buttons does it have? If the answer to that is more than three, protest. Argue with your wife if you have to. Sleep on the couch that night. Trust me, the argument will be easier to deal with.

CHAPTER 6

Goldie Dies

We'd gotten Logan a pet turtle at the Sweet Tater Festival a couple of years ago. It was the size of a silver dollar and came with about a 3x6 plastic terrarium. Logan loved him, at first anyway. He named the turtle Goldie for some reason (we tried to get him to name it one of the ninja turtle names, like his then favorite Michelangelo.)

We wound up sort of ignoring Goldie after a few weeks. I kept up the task of feeding him from a little bag of food given to us when we bought him. The bag lasted two years. Once it had gone, I started trying pieces of vegetable which he barely touched and finally bought him a little canister of freeze-dried tiny shrimp. I let Logan sprinkle a few in there the first time.

Nikki and I had come up with an idea: We'd let Goldie, who sat in his terrarium on the window sill in the kitchen for the past year or so, be placed in Logan's charge. It had become hard to remember him, and with everything going on we were left with that option or to release him into the wild. Logan was to feed him every other day (supervised by one of us, of course) and he was not to take him out of his home. I would help clean his home every now and then. Logan readily agreed to this, even when we told him that if he fails to take good care of the turtle, we were going to set it free.

Logan never got a chance to prove himself with the turtle. A few days after we made the agreement, before we could get Goldie a bigger terrarium and a place to put him in Logan's room, the little guy passed away. I noticed he hadn't moved in the past two days, and the little shrimp lay uneaten and swollen in the water beneath his feet. I told Nikki, and a cloud passed over her eyes as she realized we were going to have to tell Logan soon.

We told him after his second day of school. Logan, being a young child, has no experience with grief. He went through all the stages of grief in a matter of about ten minutes. The first thing he said, after looking at us with a wrinkled brow, was "Where is he? I want to see him!" In his voice was anger. He'd just gone through the Shock, Denial, and Anger phases all at once. The Bargaining phase was in there too, as he seemed to want to see for himself. Maybe Goldie wasn't really dead...

I pointed to the window sill above the kitchen sink. Logan had walked over there already by the time I could point. He stopped just in front of the sink and stared at the terrarium, and then turned back to face us.

"I think I'm gonna cry…" And before he could finish the word "cry," cry he did. That first wail had so much power behind it that he had to gasp for air after. He walked over to his mom and fell into her arms, crying harder than I've ever seen him cry.

I felt a little prick in the corners of my eyes as well. Nikki teared up as he cried in her arms.

One of the hardest lessons a child can learn is that of death, and it's one that doesn't get learned all at once. Logan, after crying it out for a few minutes, was back to his old self again. He'd reached the last stage of grief: Acceptance. One day he'll go through those stages a lot slower, once age and experience build his life for him.

But Goldie will always be his first.

CHAPTER 7

Its morning time, and baby is crying. Got up. Found bottle. Washed bottle. Got bottle ready. Filled with warm water. Shook the bottle for a good minute.

Never put formula in bottle.

CHAPTER 8

The Blueto Ultimatum

My son has a lot of toys. My son is also very particular about his toys. He was given a large stuffed puppy dog about two years ago by a family friend, and he's kept this stuffed dog in his room - usually on his bed - ever since.

One weekend we were all sort of lounging around in the master bedroom, hanging out and goofing off and doing a whole lot of nothing. Logan darted in and out of the room wielding various toys like his Minecraft sword or the bolt-action Nerf rifle he'd gotten a couple of birthdays ago, and he laughed and played and was as loud and rowdy as he could be. I think he is constantly testing our limits. He wants to see how loud or hyper he can get before one of us blows a gasket and sends him to his room.

The truth is I probably handle his hyperactivity better than Nikki. This is not a good thing. I'm not proud of it. See, I like playing with Logan, and I often stoop to the same six-year-old level that he's on. I'll argue with him. I'll egg him on. This tends to get me in the adult version of time-out on a semiregular basis.

So there we were sitting on the bed playing with Abby, when Logan bursts through the door. "His name is Pluto!" he proclaims, and holds the blue puppy up for everyone to see.

Now, I wasn't trying to start a situation here. I still maintain that. I was flexing the dad-joke section of my brain when I answered him: "You should call him Blueto instead, since he's blue."

A harmless statement. Not even a joke, really, just a mildly humorous suggestion that I thought might draw a smile from the kid. I figured he'd have found it way funnier than I did.

Not so. He thought for a brief moment and then reached his conclusion. "No, it's Pluto."

"Are you sure?" I pressed, for some reason. "It should be Blueto since he's blue. See?" I motion toward the dog to illustrate my obvious point.

"No, I want it to be Pluto." Logan said. And that should've been the end of it.

Spoiler Alert: it wasn't.

"I'm gonna call him Blueto." I said.

His eyebrows descended like storm clouds over his eyes. He lowered his head and exhaled. He was a bull about to charge. "His name is Pluto!" He said through gritted teeth.

I raised my hands in surrender. "Okay okay, Blueto it is."

He roared and charged. I let him knock me backwards onto the bed, and we wrestled for a few minutes. We argued back and forth, until finally he roared again in frustration and left the room.

"Logan," I called to him, "Don't be mad that the dog's name is Blueto." Logan returned wielding a foam Minecraft sword. I say foam, but this thing is no pool noodle. The ridges are 8-bit jagged, and the thing is stiff enough to cause some pain if the swing is properly placed.

"What's his name?" Logan calls again and again as he delivers a barrage of sword strikes on my backside.

"Blueto!" I call from beneath the comforter (an object which is not holding up to its definition, I might add). "His name is Blueto!"

Logan growls and pummels me with the sword. I take a few good strikes to the buttocks before he tires. He walks back to the bedroom door and stands there glaring at me.

"Okay, y'all are getting a little too rough. We're going to the living room," my wife says and picks our daughter up. They exit the battle zone.

By this point I have committed. I can't physically bring myself to say "Pluto." To me, every time I answer with "Blueto" it seems funnier and funnier. And so, I press on.

"Okay okay, Logan. You want me to say it?" I ask.

"Yes." He answers. I can see a glimmer of hope in his eyes.

"Logan, he's not gonna say it," Nikki calls from the living room.

"Say it." Logan demands anyway.

I start to smile and I see the faintest of grins dance on the corner of his mouth before he snaps it tight again. "Say his name is Pluto."

"I'm telling you Logan, he's not gonna say it." Nikki calls.

"The dog's name," I say slowly, drawing out the suspense, "is…" Silence. Logan's eyes burn holes through me. "Blueto."

"Aaaaahhh!" Logan shouts and throws his hands up. He walks back to his room fuming. I chuckle to myself for a moment. Have I taken it too far? Probably. It's off the rails now, though. The train of sensibility has not only left the station, it has careened down the tracks at suicide speeds, its brake lever broken, its massive weight charging it forward at an unstoppable pace. I simply can not say Pluto. It would violate some inner code in me that I shouldn't even have. I felt like a kid again pestering my sister and it being harder to stop the more I knew it was annoying her.

In all honesty I probably deserved a good kick in the nuts. Then and now.

So I was sitting there at the edge of the bed reminiscing about how much of an asshole I am when Logan walked back into the room, turned, and closed the door behind him, effectively sealing us off from the rest of the house. He turned back to me and that's when I noticed the Nerf gun. He slipped a foam bullet into the chamber, shoved the bolt-action lever forward, snapped it back and folded it down in a few swift motions. I half smiled as I watched him do this. He smiled too. Then he lifted the gun and a barrel of yellow plastic was staring at me from only two feet away. Logan's eyes locked on me in a dead stare. His smile fell. So did my own.

I was a sitting duck.

Logan's eyebrows raised. "What's his name?" He asked, his finger twitching on the trigger...

I'm a lot of things, but I ain't no coward. Only the slightest nervous gulp escaped my lips as I gave my answer.

The freakin' dog's name is Blueto.

Moral Of The Story: Maybe don't be an asshole to your kids, or you just may take a bullet to the chest, like I did.

CHAPTER 9

Wordsmithing and Fluids

It's inevitable that when you have a child you will come in contact with more poop, pee, puke, drool, spoiled milk, and mashed up gobs of food than you have ever encountered before. There's a whole new world out there of disgusting fluids, solids, and semi-solids just waiting for you to stick your hand in them. Even better, you usually have to pay more attention to the various stuff that comes out of your baby in order to keep a check on their health. You have to *look* at the poop. Examine it. Things that wouldn't get a second glance when it comes from your own body suddenly become a scientific study once it exits your baby.

Observe:

"Hey, did she poop?" Your wife calls from the living room as you change your daughter's diaper.

"Uh, yeah." You say.

"What's it like?"

You think: *What do you mean 'What's it like?' It's like a skunk sprayed a bowl of beef stew that's been sitting in the sun for a week, and then someone dumped it into an absorbent bag. Is that what you want to hear?*

"Uh, well…" You begin.

"What's the consistency? She's had diarrhea lately."

Oh, now we're talking. This is a question of poop viscosity. You got this. "Um, well today it's kind of like potato salad made with brown mustard and too much milk."

Pause.

"So, it's not solid?"

You have to look again. "No, kinda mushy."

"But not totally wet, right?"

Another peek. "I guess you could say semi-solid." And from that information we know that the baby is on the mend. Poops are solidifying. Who ever knew that would be such a joyous occasion?

That wasn't a real conversation between my wife and I, but it isn't too far off (let's just say I'm gonna keep that potato salad analogy in my back pocket for later use). It's a good idea of how such exchanges can go. You need to know some descriptive adjectives and metaphors, man! Is it the consistency of Elmer's glue or Play-doh? Is it thick like Greek yogurt or is it the runny kind? Does the diaper feel swollen with pee, or just mildly squishy, or is it completely dry? Is your baby teething? Wanna know how to tell? Rivers of drool spilling from her bottom lip at all times, enough to make you fear her dehydration. (How much drool fits in that tiny body anyway?)

Another fun fact: it doesn't stop once they're older and potty trained. Digestive problems in your kid? Time to examine some turds. Does it burn when they pee? Let's check the color of their urine, maybe they drank too much Coke. Fall on the playground and skinned their hands and knees? Prepare for blood and copious amounts of screaming while you apply band-aids.

As a horror fan, one of my favorite films is *Evil Dead 2*. In that movie the main character, Ash, shoots holes in the walls of his cabin while trying to destroy his possessed, severed hand. The hand scuttles through the walls like a rat and whenever it makes noise Ash fires at it. He finally hits paydirt when a thin dribble of blood streams out of the last hole. He laughs in triumph. That is, until the thin dribble begins to build in strength until it is a full-on jet of liquid pummeling his face. From the other holes in the wall more blood erupts, turning his cabin living room into the most gruesome water park ever seen. The blood changes color, becomes black. Every orifice in the cabin is oozing this sloppy, black mess. Ash stumbles around, pinballing back and forth between jets of gross liquid while trying to gain his balance. When I stop to think about it, being a dad is kind of like being Ash in that cabin: standing there with only one hand free, panic distorting your face, not knowing where the next eruption will come from and just having to wait for the inevitable blast of baby fluid to knock you on your ass.

 Moral of the Story: New dads, prepare yourselves. Fluids are coming.

CHAPTER 10

Logan Quotes

<u>June 22, 2018</u>

Logan wrote his name on his hand with a dry erase marker while sitting in his car seat. He showed us, and we told him he wasn't supposed to write on himself. He said, "That way if my hand crawls off people will know to bring it back to me."

<u>August 3, 2018</u>

"What happens to a cow when you tip him over?" Logan asks on our way back from Huntsville, where we'd just picked up his uniforms for his first year at Sacred Heart.

"I don't know. What?" Nikki asks.

"Its four wieners shoot out milk."

April 19, 2019

"Mom, I need you." Logan calls.
Nikki finds him in the bathroom.
"How can I itch my butt if I can't itch my butt?" He asks.

September 1, 2019

We were riding around on a Sunday, exploring. We wound up driving through a subdivision called Phelan East. As we rode around, Logan said: "Guys, this is just like the place we lived in the old house. When Arlo got out and went into some lady's bush!'
(context: Arlo is our dog)

July 8, 2020

"A drink is just like trying to eat a hot dog, but you drink it." - Logan

October 9th, 2021

We're playing HORSE on his junior basketball goal on the driveway. Logan had an H-O. He leaned against my car and said "I'm about to rake this garden, with my HO."

CHAPTER 11

A Chungus Among Us

Words are funny...

Every now and then my kid will say something that makes me realize how out of touch I am with the youth of today. Back in my day (he said from his old rocking chair, one eye trained on his immaculately manicured lawn while the other is watching the mailbox for the delivery of his AARP membership card) we had slang words, most of which I don't even remember now. Some of the milder ones were the surfer-stoner words like "gnarly" or "tubular" or "wicked," ushered into our vocabularies via *The Teenage Mutant Ninja Turtles*, or the Bart Simpson inspired one-liners like "Don't have a cow man," or "Eat my shorts." If we referred to someone we didn't like, they were a dork or a dweeb, and a dumb person could be called an airhead. In arguing with friends or enemies, you might suggest that they "take a chill pill" or "chill out." After *Terminator 2* was released in '92, the youth of America became just a touch more fluent in Spanish when the term "Hasta la vista, baby," was introduced.

The nineties rolled on. By the latter part of that decade, if you were a guy that lived at home witcha mama and didn't make no money, there was a word for you. You were a scrub. Your home became your crib. Things that were cool, or "gnarly" a decade ago, were now considered "dope." If you ganked something in the late nineties, that meant you stole it.

The explosion of R&B and rap in those times gave birth to all sorts of random syllables that were thrown together to form words which might mean something totally different than their original intent. Years before, Michael Jackson talked us into believing the word "bad" actually meant good, and we went along with that for a few decades. "Phat" meant Pretty Hot And Tempting, not overweight. If you were "tripping", that didn't mean you were having trouble walking, it meant you weren't acting right or you were out of line. You were actin' a fool, if you will.

Being a lily white southern kid who had lived his entire life in a small town in Alabama, I didn't use a lot of those terms but they were definitely in my lexicon. Everyone knew them, especially if you were a teenager. My parents, however, had to think kids had invented a new language or something. There must have been a revolving carousel of frowns and befuddled expressions rolling across their faces whenever kids talked.

It hasn't changed today. Well, it has changed in one way I guess: I am now the confused parent. Through the early 2000's I followed along with the slang of the time. I know what YOLO means, for example. I know that ratchet doesn't necessarily just refer to a device that loosens bolts; it now means "wretched" as well. I was a meme connoisseur for a few years there, and was able to keep up with pop culture following the trends created by that medium. You get past the year 2010 or so, though, and I start to feel a little two-thousand and late. That world began to mean less and less to me, without me even realizing it.

So that brings us to the present. A few weeks ago Logan was playing in our bedroom. We were preparing to go somewhere, and Abby and I were sitting on the bed while

Logan engaged in his usual routine of darting in and out and talking a little too loudly about any number of random subjects that popped into his head. This day, he introduced us to a new word.

"I'm a big chungus!" He shouted as he hopped around on the bed.

Nikki leaned back from her station in front of the mirror in our bathroom. "That's the third time he's used that word today." She said.

My interest was piqued. "What's a chungus, Logan?" I almost giggled at the word as I asked.

He just shrugged and mumbled some response that sounded like "I don't know" minus all the consonants.

"Sort of sounds like..." I trailed off, and waited for Nikki to lean back into frame again. When she did we shared a grin. Let's just say both of us have found certain urban dictionary words and phrases rather funny, and this one sounded like it might belong to a certain group of definitions that would relate to the sexual experience. Off to the internet I went, on a search for the almighty chungus.

"What's wrong with chungus?" Logan asked while I searched on my phone for the meaning.

"We're just trying to find out what it means." Nikki said. "We don't want you to be saying it if it's a bad word."

"Chungus isn't a bad word, it's just a big fat thing."

My mind raced as I tried to find the word. Any number of hideously inappropriate definitions found their way into my thoughts. If it was as bad as I feared, I'd have to find out where he heard it and tell him why he shouldn't say it, and the worst part was that I was going to have to do it without laughing.

It is no secret that I find it hilarious when a kid says things they shouldn't say. In my opinion bad words are funny and that's all there is to it, and it's even funnier when a kid says them. Having said that I do understand the need to teach my kid which words are and are not acceptable to say.

Finally I found a definition for chungus. Google led me, as I had feared, straight to the Urban Dictionary.

Basically, a chungus is a giant, overweight rabbit that destroys things. Images that popped up during the search portrayed a hefty Bugs Bunny, a lazy smile pushing up his fat cheeks under dazed, stupid eyes.

Part of me felt relief. An equal part of me wondered how in the skittle-tits a word like that, with a definition like that, even existed. Sure we had our slang when I was a kid, but not once in my childhood do I ever remember feeling the need to reference and overweight destructive bunny in my day-to-day conversation. To be honest I'm kind of disappointed that that never came up...

I read the definition out so we could all hear it. Nikki and I shared confused glances, but all in all thought it was pretty funny.

"Why didn't y'all want me to say it?" Logan asked.

"We thought it might be a bad word." Nikki said.

"You mean like B-" Logan began, and cut himself off because he knew the word he was about to say was a bad word.

Guess who else knew?

"Like what?" I ask him.

"The B word." He said.

"What B word?" I feigned ignorance. *Come on, say it!* I thought.

He paused for a moment, looked at both of us across the room, and said it. "Bitch."

"Logan!" Nikki said. I could see the smile in her eyes though. When Logan turned from me I chuckled.

Look, it's funny, okay? It's funny and it's not hurting anybody, and I will think it's funny for the rest of my life. We made sure he knows not to say that word, but I suspect

I will always ask him to repeat himself if he accidentally lets one slip, just so I can hear him say it again.
Don't judge me.

<u>Moral of the story:</u> I guess you shouldn't teach your kids bad words, or ask them to repeat them. And keep up with the lingo. You never know when your kid might be saying something that sounds cutesy, but is actually slang for some devious sex act. Don't believe me? Just take a stroll through the pages of the Urban Dictionary.

CHAPTER 12

Mine-craft

"Why did you put that there? You're destroying the house! I just built that."

"Fine, if I can't put that there I'll go build my own and you won't be invited!"

"You've already taken over this one. Somehow the living room is now a stable with two horses in it. There are twenty dogs in my bedroom. There are twenty *beds* in my bedroom. And why are all these parrots in cages? I can't even walk through the place. You stay here and do what you want, and I'll go build another house."

Above: The main area of Logan Land. It's a bit chaotic, but it has it's charms.

"But I want to come too!"

"Okay, but this one's gonna be mine okay? You have to build it like I say."

Two blocky characters hop and trot through a similarly blocky world, away from the jumble of blocky glass and blocky stone and blocky dirt. In a way the world resembles a 3D, open world version of the original Super Mario Bros. game, minus the giant green pipes. The two characters choose a spot on a hill, and one begins clearing blocks so that the surface is flat. While he's doing that, the other one begins to build about three feet from him.

"What are you doing?"

"I'm building a clubhouse."

"I don't want a clubhouse."

"This is my part of the house."

"But I said this is my area and you have to build it like I want."

"This isn't on your property. This is on my land beside yours. I'm building a clubhouse."

"Okay well if you're gonna do that I'm gonna make changes to it when you're not playing."

"Why would you do that?! That's not fair!"

"Well it's not fair that you're building on my land either, is it?"

"But I'm on my land!"

"You know what? Fine. Build the clubhouse. But you can't build in my house."

A few minutes pass. The foundation of the house is completed, and the character that is building the house begins setting rows of blocks that will become walls. The second character, having completed his clubhouse just a few Minecraft blocks away, wants something else to do. So he climbs down from his elevated clubhouse and hops onto the flat surface of the foundation that character #1 has been clearing for thirty minutes.

He begins digging.

"What are you doing?"

"I'm building a basement."

"I don't recall asking for a basement."

"It needs a basement, and that will be my part of the house."

"But this is my house!"

"Not all of it! Some of it needs to be mine!"

And the cycle repeats.

Above:My house in the center, with an unplanned basement beneath (unseen) and a wooden clubhouse with random white sticks littering the base, and apparently a light show going on behind the house.

Does any other adult ever hear themselves argue with their child and realize that their mental and emotional capacity shrinks to match that of the six-year-old boy with whom they're arguing? By now it's probably evident that this exchange is happening between my son and me. We've played Minecraft together off and on for at least two years now I'd guess, and we always have fun. We do not, however, always get along. And I'll be damned if I don't revert to a whiny little bitch when I can't build this fictional house on a glorified child's game to my exact structural and architectural specifications.

The worst part about this, I always realize later, is that my son is wanting to play with me right then. This is potential for some good quality time I'll have with him, time that won't last forever. How many more years will I have of him destroying what I built in that game before he decides he's too cool to play Minecraft anymore? Will I still turn the game on and stroll through our Frankenstein monster of a house after he's given up playing it? I suspect there will be a time in the not too distant future when I'll be begging my boy to build a stupid room to house his towers of caged parrots and stalls of skeleton horses and potion-making tables. I mean, who doesn't want a world with a house built like a giant chicken with a doorway for an ass?

Above: Logan's "chicken house." The butt's the doorway. I do like this one

a lot.

<u>Moral of the Story:</u> Let the kid build the ridiculous room onto your playhouse, you near forty-year-old squall tit.

CHAPTER 13

Prey at Dawn

My wife and I lay in bed facing each other. It's just past 4 a.m. Our eyes are mostly closed. We peek at each other from time to time.

A line from Jurassic Park is rolling through my head, and I will the thought towards my wife. I hope she has the psychic ability to pick up on the message.

She can't see us if we don't move.

That's the line from the movie, as the T-Rex is sweeping the scene for hints of the presence of Dr. Alan Grant, Lex, and Tim after it has destroyed the Jeep.

On this night a fourteen month old baby is the roving monster. She'd awakened screaming in the middle of the night, her nose running and her chest slightly congested. My wife volunteered me to go get her so I crept through the house to her room, opened her door, and lifted her out of the crib.

Nikki had whispered to me as I'd exited our room "Don't talk to her when you go in. Just pick her up and bring her in here." That may sound mean, but it's the only way to hold on to the thin veil of sleepiness that the baby is still clinging to. If we were to talk to her or turn on the light everything would be ruined. Once we were in bed and she had been laid comfortably between us, we couldn't open our eyes. She had to believe we'd gone back to sleep or she'd be awake, and nothing would stop her from keeping us awake. The illusion would be destroyed.

That was the theory, anyway, and a damn good one it was. It has worked in the past. This morning, though, Abby didn't want to go back to sleep. It seems she's gotten smarter.

Clever girl...

I crack my eyelids to take a peek. The room is dark, but my eyes have adjusted and indirect light has softened the shadows just enough so I can see the silhouette of my daughter. She sits on the bed, looking from me to her mom, waiting on one of us to break.

We're being hunted...

She leans in towards her mom, her face mere inches away. I can see Nikki's eyelids twitching. *Hold it*, I think. *Be strong.*

The baby raises her hand and swings. It connects with Nikki's cheek, and a little *smack!* breaks the silence of the room. Nikki flinches slightly, but her eyes remain closed.

I stifle a laugh and that draws attention to me. I might as well be waving a road flare.

The dark silhouette shifts, and is now hovering over my face.

"Dah!" The baby blurts, and slaps my face.

I bite my lip. The slap doesn't hurt, but it's funny as hell that we've come to this.

Go to sleep!

This time I'm trying to psychically link up to my daughter. As expected, it works about as well as a squirt gun putting out a house fire.

In the end it took about thirty minutes of pretending to sleep (and, indeed, *being* half asleep) to get the baby to give up. She eventually eased her head down onto the pillow between us and grew still. It didn't exactly stop there, though. There was one last act of defiance left in her, performed while she was asleep. She wormed her way around and ended up sleeping horizontally across the bed, her feet in my back and her head pushing Nikki's back.

We clung to the cliff edges for the remainder of the night, balancing precariously on the edges of the bed, while our daughter slept comfortably between us.

62

CHAPTER 14

I Thought It Was Something Good But It's Snot

Yesterday morning began as one of those perfect golden moments between my daughter and I. Like many mornings I was the first one awake. I took care of my morning routine (Okay okay, I had to pee. Peeing is my morning routine.) and laid back down in bed for a little while. Soon enough, our baby monitor blasts the voice of our daughter into the room. She sobs for a couple of seconds and then stops. I look past my wife to the video feed and see Abby begin to stir in her crib. Eventually she sits up and looks around her room with sleepy eyes. That's my cue.

I get up, walk into her room, she smiles at me as I pick her up, and we head to the kitchen to get her morning cup of milk. Once the lid to the sippy cup has been secured we amble back to the bedroom where I sit her on the bed beside me and we chill out. It's the weekend, after all.

She babbles, I babble back. She drinks her milk and pats the bed sheets and looks around. Her mom lies asleep beside us. Every now and then Abby slaps at her mom's back to wake her up, but it doesn't work.

The sun creeps through the bedroom window, casting a subtle golden light into the room. As it climbs higher the light gets stronger, and ignites the fine fibers of corn silk hair on my daughter's head. Her chubby cheeks are crested with sunlight from the window behind her. She looks up at me with a content smile. She leans back to drink more of her milk, and I cup my hand around the back of her head to keep her from leaning too far back and falling. She pulls the sippy cup out of her mouth and looks at me. I smile at her.

"I love you Abs." I say.

Kind of a sweet moment, right?

Have you ever used one of those hand-held misters? The spray bottles with the little fan attached to it? You pull the trigger and the fan spits a cloud of vaporized water into your face, coating you with a cool sheen that is refreshing on a hot summer day. Well, it's slightly less refreshing when you're in your bedroom, and the liquid that is scattered across your cheeks isn't water but baby snot.

I caught the look in her eyes less than a second before the sneeze hit. The first wave misted my face with globules of mucus. The second wave shot an earthworm-sized snot rocket from my daughter's right nostril that flopped over her mouth and began oozing its way toward her chin. The third and final wave pushed the booger rope further out of her nose, and she smiled that adorable OPEN MOUTHED smile at me once the sneezing fit had ceased. The slime from her nose sagged into her mouth.

"Oh no! No no no..." I say as I look for any available napkin or tissue. Normally my nightstand is a Swiss army knife of useless junk: books, remotes, earphones, mail, a cup or two. I take a quick stock of items near me. There are no absorbent materials. Finally I accept what I already knew was the answer the minute I saw the goop hanging from her nose: I would have to sacrifice my shirt.

I keep hold of the back of her head, work my hand beneath my shirt, and make a sort of puppet out of my thumb and pointer finger. I clamp my shirt-covered fingers onto Abby's nose before she even knows what hit her, squeeze, and swipe. It gets about half of it, so I have to do it again. This time, though, my daughter is ready. She takes evasive action as I struggle to hold the mouth of my shirt puppet - now smeared with boogers - open. After she jukes me a few times I catch her nose with my hand puppet (let's just call him Booger McSnottersen) over her nose and mouth and make a quick sweep across the bottom half of her face. I get it all that time, for the most part. Later there will probably be a crusted coat across her mouth, nose, and chin, like the cracked ground of Death Valley, but the hard part is over. All it costed was a perfectly good t-shirt. Booger McSnottersen is a mess, to say the least.

<u>Moral of the Story:</u>

"Tissues are your friend. Keep them everywhere.

(with menacing eyes and deep voice) EVERYWHERE."
- Booger McSnottersen

CHAPTER 15

Logan the Barber

It was a Thursday night. Nikki and I had been in the living room, eating supper, watching TV, and tending to Abby, and Logan was in his room playing and watching his TV. Every now and then, per usual, he would dart out of his room, run down the hall, be silly for a bit, and go back to his room. At one of these moments I was standing in front of my recliner and he was play fighting with me. Something looked strange about him, but I couldn't immediately figure out what it was. I finally realized it looked like he'd parted his hair in the middle, but as I looked closer I noticed the "part" was actually a missing patch of hair in the center of his forehead. Already knowing the answer to my question, I still hoped my eyes were just tricking me.

"Logan did you cut your hair?"

He froze. A guilty grin began to crease his lips.

I noticed a couple of other places where he'd cut along the side of his face. Nikki and I looked at each other. Nikki called him over to her and rubbed her hands through his hair, searching for places he'd cut. "Why did you do that?" She asked. Neither of us were exactly getting on to him, but there was a stern tone to our voices and he started to get nervous. Nikki took a picture of him and showed it to him, and Logan started to cry, saying he hated it. I think he then realized exactly what he had done.

He had to go to school Friday with that hair. Nikki used hair gel and styled it as well as she could, and that weekend we took him to the barber shop and they basically had to give him a buzz cut to fix it. He ended up liking the buzz cut.

I can't remember if it was that same day or the next day, but I asked him why he thought he could cut his own hair and he looked at me and said "You do it all the time!" He'd seen me trimming my beard, and he'd seen my dad cutting my hair, so I guess he thought it was normal for someone to cut their own hair. Haha!

CHAPTER 16

The Christmas Showcase Showdown

At the end of every episode on the classic game show The Price Is Right, two contestants have to duke it out to win one of two showcases. One will have a washer/dryer set and a one-night-stay at a Motel 6 in Utah or something, where the other will have a new Ford Mustang, a sailboat and an all-expenses-paid trip to the Bahamas. One always seemed to be crap compared to the other.

As a parent of two kids you play the Showcase on a daily basis, usually minus the awesome prizes. Sometimes it's choosing between a dirty diaper and a Nerf bullet to the left testicle. Most of the time it's more mundane, like would you rather sit at home and watch two hours of some twenty-something kid play video games on YouTube with your son, or take your daughter to her doctor's appointment?

Oh, and you can't say "neither." That gets you into the secret, third Showcase which includes one of the previous two showcases plus a healthy dose of dread as you await the argument that will come later because you decided to be a smartass. (To give myself a little credit here, I would never say I didn't want to take my child to the doctor, or spend time with my kid by watching YouTube videos, but sometimes neither is really appealing).

On Christmas Eve we went to my grandmother's house. My family on my dad's side is enormous. My grandparents had eight children, and those children produced sixteen grandchildren. Now there are almost a dozen great-grandchildren. You throw in a few family friends and some in-law relatives and that's about fifty people crammed into one house. I have spent every Christmas Eve of my entire life surrounded by these people, and I have a great time doing it.

With two kids in tow, though, a few challenges arise. I wish I was one of those lizards with the roving, cone shaped eyes that move independently. That way I could see both kids at once. Instead, it usually devolves into my wife watching one kid while I watch the other. It usually works well.

This Christmas Eve, though, I got a little confident. Surely with so many people around I wouldn't have to keep eyes on them the whole night, right? After all, the house is full of adults, and the kids are occupied with other kids. At least Logan is fine by himself for a little while, surely.

With this illusion in mind I saunter into the kitchen where my brother, two cousins, and an uncle stand and talk. I nudge my way into the conversation. We all share a few laughs and carry on the way we always do, and at one point my eyes lock onto my wife's. She's apparently been trying to wave me down for ten minutes.

I do the whole raise-my-eyebrows-and tilt-my-head-back routine. *What's up?*

"I need you over here." She calls through the noise.

I saunter back.

"You can either change Abby's diaper or help Logan in the bathroom. He's calling me from the door and she needs a diaper change."

The Showcase presents itself.

I can see clearly what's behind door number one: a diaper change (though I don't know the severity of the soilage of said diaper). What I don't know is what's behind door number two, although there is a twinge of understanding that door number two most likely has to do with "number two." Still, I can only speculate. I'm closer to door number two so that 's what I chose.

Door#2: The son in the bathroom.

It turns out Logan was having some digestive difficulties and needed some encouragement, but by the time I tapped on the door and let myself in he'd completed his duties (hehehe). I told him to go ahead and flush and we'd be on our merry way.

He'd been coughing for the past two days, though, and after he'd flushed the toilet a fit of hacking sputtered in his chest. Eventually the coughs became too much. Logan leaned over.

Oh Jeez, he's gonna...

And it came up.

And it was red.

I tried to stay calm. All kinds of ailments, diseases, and physical problems ran through my mind for the next few seconds. Why is it red? Please God don't let it be blood.

"Um, Logan?" I frowned as I studied the pinkish brown blob in the toilet. "Why is it-"

"I ate a cookie earlier."

Oh thank God! Right after he said it I remembered he'd asked for the cookie just a half an hour earlier. It had red icing.

My son was not puking blood.

I told Nikki about the vomit and the alarming color, being quick to remind her he'd had a cookie with red icing not long ago. We asked Logan not to run around as much. We figured he'd gotten hot and that made him momentarily sick to his stomach, and I think we were right. He hasn't gotten sick since.

So that was my Showcase: Pee diaper or poop with a dollop of red puke. I didn't come away with a new car or a trip to a tropical paradise, but on the bright side my son was not coughing up blood. There's always a silver lining.

<u>Moral of the Story:</u> There's not one. Whenever a Showcase presents itself, just choose one quickly and move on. You may think you're choosing the path of least resistance, but then someone vomits and all bets are off.

CHAPTER 17

Ghosts of Christmases Past

Two years ago we - strike that, "Santa" - got Logan a Hot Wheels Super Ultimate Garage as his big gift for Christmas. On the side of the main tower clung a toy gorilla that Logan referred to as King Kong. This giant pile of snap-together plastic cost just shy of two hundred dollars, and it was all Logan talked about when we asked him what he wanted Santa to bring. It had to be under the tree.

So Christmas Eve of 2017 rolled around. The box this thing came in was about the size of the monolith on *2001: A Space Odyssey,* and I had the pleasure of wrestling that box into a coating of wrapping paper that was red, white, and silver and would have looked right at home with a Budweiser logo on it. The minute Logan walked into the room the following morning he pointed at the box. "That's the King Kong thing!" He said. It was the last gift he opened that year, and he squealed with excitement as he tore through the beer paper... er... wrapping paper. The look on his face as he opened the present told us we had done our job.

Logan played with it for a couple of months after we'd set it up in his room, but over time it became a really colorful place to set cups and books and other forms of debris that always seems to congregate in a child's room. It spent the next year and a half being a dust catcher. One of the orange strips that connected the garage to a winding, loopy off ramp disappeared. The spaceship that perched atop the highest level of it vanished into a pit filled with balls and cars and Nerf guns and action figures. The massive thing withstood the weather of a hyperactive young boy for two years, but now it squatted in the corner like an abandoned building awaiting a demolition crew.

This past week Nikki and I moved that heap of joy out of Logan's room and onto our front porch. It's destination: the thrift store. For some reason that I couldn't quite pinpoint at the time, it bothered me that we were getting rid of it. It was bulky, it took up space, it wasn't used. There was no reason to keep it. Logan wasn't even all that upset that it was going away.

I guess that was the problem. I was certain Logan would be attached to the toy garage because he'd wanted it so bad, but he'd had it for two years. He's only six years old. That was a third of his lifetime ago. The garage had gotten its fifteen minutes with Logan, and it was time for it to move on.

I thought back on Christmases when I was young. The memories that gathered in my mind were blizzards of voices and laughter and chairs sliding on the floor and silverware on plates and the crackle of wrapping paper. I thought of fifty people laughing in a tiny house my grandparents had owned for half a century. I thought of counting houses decked out with Christmas lights on rides home after dark, and I thought of mom making us sing carols in the car along with the radio station. I remember being seven years old and seeing a red blinking light in the sky - no doubt an airplane - at my other grandparents' house. I believed with every bone in my body that it was Rudolph's nose as he guided a sleigh through the night sky. I thought of being unable to go to sleep on Christmas Eve, and wondering when Santa would show up. I thought of waking up at two in the morning with my brother and creeping into the living room to see the presents, and the sheer torture mom forced on us by making us wait until she and my dad were awake before we started opening them. All that came drifting back when I thought of Christmases past, but not a single thought was given to individual gifts I'd received.

In the end I decided that the Super Ultimate Garage, now taking up all my porch space, could go on to its next adventure with my blessing. The conclusion I reached is that it's okay for your kid to blow through life giving passing glances to the toys he loved yesterday. The toys, the material things, are not what he'll think about when he looks back to these times in his life.

I hope he looks back and remembers family movie nights watching *Home Alone* or *Elf* or *The Grinch*. I hope he remembers his parents driving his sister and him through the Christmas light display at Sportsman's Lake, and playing with his cousins at the family party on Christmas Eve. I hope he remembers opening gifts with his sister in their pajamas on Christmas morning, drinking hot chocolate, and eating candy from his stocking.

One day I hope he'll set his own child's toys outside when it's time to let them go, and memories of what made Christmas so important will flood through him. If we've done a good enough job as parents, those memories won't center around a toy Hot Wheels garage, but around the people he loves and the times spent with them.

CHAPTER 18

Barrel O' Monkeys

I'm not going to gross you out here. I've done that too much with past episodes. This is a safe place. Just know that I walked through our front door the other day holding my child and, about three minutes later, she hurled. Repeatedly. She and I were bathed in it, let's say, and I'll leave the imagery at that.

Now, on to the meat 'n potatoes of this post (no, that's not a reference to the copious amounts of puke, or what my daughter ate to cause such an outburst, so quit thinking about those disgusting things). Much like any other given moment in the span of my time as a parent, I didn't know what to do. I stood there and thankfully remembered to lean her forward as the event took place so that she didn't choke, but after the deed was done I became Neanderthal Luke (See chapter 1) searching my cave for a towel, a washcloth, a stack of napkins, or just a simple clue as to how in the hell I was going to begin to clean this mess up.

I started the cleanup by setting my daughter down and taking her shirt off. It didn't occur to me until after I'd started to do this that hey, she probably doesn't want me to rake a puke covered shirt across her face as I remove it. Probably didn't want any of it to get stuck in her eyebrows either. Hindsight is always 20/20. With my daughter screaming and her shirt gone, I pick her up and tip-toe around the mess. I spot a pack of baby wipes on top of the microwave. I'm saved.

Here's where I lose it.

With my one free hand I work the package open and I pinch the top wipe with my fingernails. I pull, and a wipe comes out. It has a friend. And that one has a friend. And the next one. These friggin' wipes are playing Barrel O' Monkeys with me and I'm looking like a half-ass magician pulling a never-ending string of tissues out of the package while my baby sobs in my other arm. Mind you, I'm still covered in puke at this point.

I then do what most any man would do. I get mad. I pull faster, and wipe after wipe is jerked from the bag until finally they spill over the side of the microwave and a few drift to the floor. When the chain is broken, I snap the string of remaining wipes like a bullwhip and I'm left with one. The others scatter into the air and come to rest uselessly at my feet. I wipe Abby's nose, mouth, and eyebrows. I carry her to our bedroom where I lay her down to change her. It is only then that I remembered my shirt and jacket had been, shall we say, severely soiled. I may or may not have dripped said soilage down the hall as I hurried to get Abby cleaned up. Luckily my wife stepped out of the bathroom as I changed the baby, and Nikki wasn't nearly as helpless. Between the two of us we eventually got the mess cleaned up.

We've put men on the moon. We put robots on Mars, and others into orbit around the moons of Jupiter and Saturn and God knows where else. We've sent two satellites on an interstellar flight that began in the 70's and they are still sending data today. We can split an atom. We've sent men into ocean depths several miles deep. Untold thousands of obstacles were overcome in order to carry out these missions. Surely somewhere along the way someone had to figure out how two damp materials could be pulled across one another without clinging to themselves and dragging all the others along for the ride. Is there anyone in any scientific field that knows how to design a package of baby wipes that doesn't make you look like the world's saddest magician when trying to rip one from the package?

<u>Moral of the Story:</u> When your baby wipes refuse to let go, it's you who must let go.
Of your rage.

CHAPTER 19

I'm Getting Old Doo Doo, Doo Doo, Doo Doo

Did you know that cool has an expiration date? I remember a time when I didn't know that...

When I got my first car, an '86 Honda Civic with a New Mexico tag and luxurious green carpet interior - and an alarm system for those who might want to steal that hunk of raw, four cylinder power - I thought I was the bees knees.

(Quick tangent: The "bees knees" phrase is thought to have derived from the word "business," as a slang word that meant something like the epitome of excellence. Other adjectives that popped up in this period of the 1920's are "the cat's pajamas," the "eel's ankles," and the "elephant's instep." Around the same time, the British came up with their own animal/anatomical part combo: the "dog's bollocks." Henceforth, since the word "bollocks" doesn't get used in the U.S. enough, I will be using that term whenever I can possibly fit it in.)

So back to what I was saying, I thought I was the dog's bollocks. I could go where I wanted. I had a sound system with a cassette player and a cassette-to-portable-CD-player converter that allowed you to play CD's through your car's tape deck. It was a sweet setup as long as you didn't hit any bumps in the road. Portable players were only meant to sit on a flat, level surface with no movement whatsoever, basically rendering them anything but portable.

I drove to school with the music screaming out of that little car. I rocked out to Sublime, The Smashing Pumpkins, Nine Inch Nails, The Deftones, maybe a little 2Pac or Dr. Dre thrown in. I drove with the windows down (I'm fairly sure the A/C was broken). I wanted to feel the music running through me, so it needed to be played at as close to max volume as my little speakers could handle. When they rattled, it was time to turn it down half a notch. Best not test the factory speakers.

I don't think I was too obnoxious with my music, but then again does an obnoxious person know they're being obnoxious? In my experience that answer is no. No they don't. I do remember a high school friend telling me they could hear my music from about three cars behind at a stoplight on the way to school, and that sounds pretty obnoxious to me. But the world was big and I was young and it was a time for excess. Strain those eardrums. Let the music course through you. In that day and age, your music was what made you cool! At least that's what I thought then.

A couple of months ago my baby daughter and I were in town together and she had a little meltdown. The drive home that day brought me to the realization that I had met the expiration date for being cool. I drove with music blaring from my car, oh yes. I got looks from people at stoplights and drew attention to myself like I had done twenty years ago. This time, though, I wasn't singing along to Rage Against The Machine's "Killing in the Name" or "March of the Pigs" by Nine Inch Nails. My phone was connected to my car, and through that phone the Youtube app played a little ditty called "Baby Shark." For those of you that know it, I'm sorry for bringing it up. For those that don't, I'm sorry for bringing it up. I hate that friggin' video.

Also, I love that video. Some angel had seen fit to post a one-hour-long version of that song on constant repeat. Abby rode the rest of the way home in relative silence, enjoying the absolutely insane monotony of that song as it repeated over and over and over and over and over and over again.

So my level of badassery has diminished over the years. I am no longer the dog's bollocks. The streets of Cullman are more likely to hear "doo doo doodoo doodoo" wafting through the air around my car than any hard rock, metal, or industrial band. Instead of feeling electrified by teenage angst I'm singing along with a family of cartoon sharks as they playfully try to eat two children.

Come to think of it that sounds pretty horrific.

<u>Moral of the Story:</u> Embrace the baby shark. By a narrow margin, it's better to hear this song on repeat than the screaming and crying of your child.

CHAPTER 20

Icicles and Spidey Senses

Some of the fondest memories from my childhood involved the colder months of the year. There was Christmas, of course. Even better, though, were the snow days that got us out of school and allowed us to head out to a solid white landscape, smothered in fifteen layers of clothes, to throw snowballs and make snow cream and all the other fun stuff we do as kids.

We'd search for the largest icicles. They were usually hanging from the eaves of the house, and if they weren't long enough to grab with a hop off the ground, then it would take a precision-thrown baseball to knock them down. We used to eat them like Popsicles. (*Side note: I had no idea Popsicle was a brand name and not the general name for any bar of ice on a stick. I got that red squiggly line under the word after I typed it, and I was like "Oh hell no, I did not misspell popsicle. Fight me, computer!" Turns out I didn't capitalize the word. That's why my computer judged me. Apparently the generic name I was looking for is "ice pops." I like Popsicle better, so that's what you're getting. Just like every carbonated beverage is a Coke, right?*)

The past couple of years have not brought much snow. They have, on occasion, brought a type of cold that can cut straight through your jeans and turn your dangly bits to ice pops. It has the ability to glue your car doors shut, and will create stalactites of ice on the bumpers of your vehicles.

About a week ago one such cold snap swept through our neighborhood overnight and left a few icicles in its wake. It was a weekday and we had gone through our morning routine. The conclusion to that routine occurs when Nikki carries Abby to her SUV, and Logan walks along with them. I watch from the door's window until they're in the car. This morning my eyes found a large, dripping icicle hanging from the side of my car just as my family were heading down the steps. That's cool, I thought. Logan will see that and he'll think it's neat. He may pick it from the car. Maybe he'll drop it on the concrete and watch it shatter, or want to save it in the freezer, or taste it like I would have done (though that one's probably a little unsanitary). All acceptable responses.

That, however, was not Logan's response. As if on cue he saw the ice and made a dash for it. Nikki and Abby were ahead of him, heading toward the back seat to strap Abby into her car seat.

I'm not sure if it's a parent thing or just a human nature thing, but there are times when things go into slow motion, times when your mind has worked something out and is desperately trying to clue you into the fact that it knows some event is about to happen. Kind of like spidey-senses. Say, when your kid is about to fall off the couch or when a ball comes flying at your head, and you react first before you even really know what's going on. Your mind has slowed it down for you, to give you time to process it.

Logan stood up from beside my car, and without even seeing his face (he was smirking, I could tell that from the back of his head. Weird, huh?) I knew what he was about to do. His elbow cocked back and his free hand went forward as if he were a pitcher about to deliver a fastball. Spidey senses tingling, I was still behind a closed door.

All I could do was watch as he launched the icicle towards Nikki and Abby. It shattered on the concrete at

Nikki's feet, causing her to jolt. She turned and admonished him, and Logan quickly apologized.

I think kids have a sort of anti-spidey-sense. If mine slows down to let me know something's wrong, Logan's seems to speed up. *Don't worry about consequences, just throw the damn thing!* his brain tells him. *Get it done before you can think about it!* He had no intentions of hurting anyone, of that I'm sure, but he didn't allow himself time to understand that he was throwing a pointy projectile at his mother and infant sister.

In the end, it really wasn't a big deal. Even if the icicle had hit them, the likelihood of an injury was maybe 0.01%. If there's any concern, it's that I need to work with him on his pitching arm if he ever wants to play baseball.

That throw needed work.

CHAPTER 21

Sippy Cups Suck (A.K.A. – The Leakening)

My daughter and I sit at a dining table. Sunlight from a perfect Spring day slants through the windows. A bird chirps from somewhere in the distance. There is laughter and merriment in the neighborhood, and Abby and I sit with smiles on our faces having a light lunch. She picks up her sippy cup and sips, ever so daintily, from it and then places it securely on the dining room table.

"Thank you father," she says, and offers a little bow of the head. "This milk is exquisite. Two percent?"

"One." I counter. "Only the best for my little angel."

"Angel indeed!" She says, smiles, and sips from her cup again. When she sits the cup down it leans and threatens to tip over, but she catches it. We share a glance after the near incident and then both chuckle heartily as if we were the ending shot of a sitcom credit sequence. Probably frozen in place and everything.

So none of that crap happened.

You know why? Because a toddler's cup is not used for drinking as an adult's cup is. It doesn't just sit on the table or the high chair tray and never move. The reality is that holding liquid is only one use for a child's sippy cup. Abby's has been used with equal measure as a hammer, a baseball, a watering can for our floors, a step stool (never goes well), a stress management tool (she throws it), and a comfort device, as sometimes she likes to just carry it around with her for no reason. We've been through at least half a dozen cups over the past six months, and I've come to a very grim conclusion.

There isn't a sippy cup on earth that doesn't leak.

I'd love to see what qualifies as a good test procedure to see if a cup is leak proof or spill proof. I picture a group of engineers standing proudly beside a table in a lab, grins and nods of approval rippling through them as one of them reaches out and gently lays their prototype sippy cup on its side. Another one keeps a timer. They stare at the cup. Ten seconds later an alarm goes off, signaling the end of their experiment. They all shake hands and congratulate each other. Job well done, right? The cup has survived ten seconds of lying on its side. One of them slaps a "Leak Proof" sticker on it and sends that baby over to the marketing department.

In my home there is no gently placing a cup on a table or floor. Half the cups we have end up lying on their side, a puddle of milk or water resting just below the lid as if the thing had seen too much and pissed itself out of fear, anxiety, or exhaustion. I have yet to find one that can survive Hurricane Abby. And Abby's a relatively calm baby! What do parents of hyper kids do?

So anyway, now I walk into Wal-Mart wearing a brown leather jacket and a dusty fedora, a bullwhip tied through my belt loop. An old man stands in the sippy cup aisle of the infant section, chain mail inexplicably covering his head, shoulders and chest. He holds an ancient sword. When I approach he wearily looks up at me.

"You must choose..." The old man says, his arm sweeping across the aisle of sippy cups. "But choose wisely. For the true leak-proof cup will bring you peace, but the false, leaky cups will take peace from you."

I step forward. My eyes roam the display of colorful plastic cups with their whimsical little pictures of ducks or elephants or Mickey Mouses printed on them. I make my choice.

I exit the aisle, proceed with my purchase and head home so Abby can test her new cup. As I leave I imagine I can hear the old knight say something, but can't quite make it out.

What he says: "He chose… poorly."

CHAPTER 22

Please

Abby has discovered the word "Please," and life will never be the same for me again. I got home from work and was sitting in my recliner. Nikki was in our bedroom and Logan was in his room. The TV was on, but it was just on the Xbox home screen.

Abby looked at it, looked at me, and pinched the air with her fingers and said "Doot doot?" That's her way of asking to watch Baby Shark (the pinches are the motions the song uses for the baby shark).

I winced. "No, not right now baby."

She pinched the air again. "Doot doot?" Then she nodded as if trying to influence me to nod in unison with her.

"No not right now."

"Peeeeese." The "s" sound was almost a "sh."

There was a sinking in my stomach. I don't know why, but I guess maybe it was because she's learning to express herself more. That and it sounded adorable. On the flip side, the dark underbelly of that coin, she's also learning how to manipulate.

Damn it.

We watched Baby Shark.

CHAPTER 23

Cabin Fever

Things have unraveled a bit at Casa Whaley. Due to the Covid-19 pandemic, My wife is working from home, and has been since last month. We have two small children (one seven-year-old, one nineteen-month-old) who are now out of school and with her all day. Some days I come home to a calm house where I'm greeted with a running hug from the baby girl, another hug from her mom, and a short but effective wrestling match with Logan, who is usually hunkered in front of a video game in a back room. Those days we accept the quarantine with a smile.

Other times my wife stands in the kitchen with her head down, palms flat on the island's surface, one eye twitching, a few strands of hair taking the Albert Einstein approach to style. She breathes slowly, deceptively calm. She stands there like she's trying to hold that boulder from the beginning of Raiders of The Lost Ark on her shoulders. At her feet confetti is scattered across the floor. As my eyes adjust I see that it's not confetti, it's Froot Loops. The living room floor is a landmine of stuffed animals, children's books, blankets, crumbs, hard plastic toys that are really fun to step on, and clothes. It doesn't take long for me to realize that at some point in the day, something has gone awry. My wife looks at me as if to dare me to say something.

I usually don't say anything.

It's at about this point that my baby girl comes trotting up to me and hugs my leg. She has no idea that anything is wrong. There's always a content smile on her lips, usually a greeting of "Hi daddy." All around her is the evidence of her destruction. This day has driven her mother to near insanity, has made her question whether or not she could go on with her work and home life in such chaos. To Abby, it's Tuesday.

The kids have their ways of dealing with the cabin fever too, though. Their daily lives have also been uprooted. As normal, one night I got settled (and by that I mean I walked through the door and stripped down to the bare minimum amount of clothes necessary to keep my dignity in front of my family) and took the baby to get her diaper changed. My first mistake was allowing her to drag the Nerf rifle along with her. I figured she'd need something to keep her distracted, and there were no bullets in it. What harm could it do?

We get back to the master bedroom. Yes, we still change Abby on our bed (if you want to know some of the earlier dangers of that, read Chapter 2). Logan is lying on the bed, watching Youtube videos on the Xbox. I lay Abby down and get to work. The first blow came from the left. A swipe of neon green and orange connected with my temple and sent a jolt of pain and shock through my head. It startled me more than it hurt me, but it was still unexpected. Before I could process what had happened, though, the second blow came. The Nerf gun bounced off my forehead.

"Abby! No!" I said, but she was already on swing number three.

My second mistake was not taking the gun away at that point.

In order to change a baby you need two hands. Those same two hands can't also fend off an attack while they are attempting to fasten the diaper around the baby's waist. I was already mid-fasten when the gun hit me, so I had no other choice but to finish the job as quickly as I could while the shots rained down. In the background I heard laughter. Logan was getting some free entertainment, it seemed, while my daughter rifle-whipped me.

All told, I really only took about five shots before she understood that she needed to stop. She's at that age where it's funny when someone says "Ouch!" Looks like her mom and I have some work to do.

As for Logan, I'll be collecting Nerf bullets for the next few days. I'll gather all the guns. Load 'em up. Wait for the perfect time to strike.

No one laughs at me.

<u>Moral of the Story:</u> Stay sane out there, people. That cabin fever's a bitch.

CHAPTER 24

The Sound and the Fuhrer

As I navigate the vast, majestic and sometimes troubled waters of dadhood, I almost always look back and think of how amazing it has been to be a part of these two kids' lives. Every day I hope I'm making a positive impact on their development. Every day they surprise me with their intellect and their kindness and their cuteness. There is, however, a dark underbelly. Case in point, yesterday afternoon my one-and-a-half-year-old daughter engaged me in hand-to-hand combat.

I accepted.

She was pissed because I had raised my voice at her after she pulled her brother's hair and tried to bite him. First I told her "No," which worked about as well as blowing bubbles into a hurricane. After she tried it again I raised my voice, saying "NO!" again, secretly hoping that would do the trick so that I didn't have to get out of my recliner (If you're thinking "What a lazy sack of bull squirt," I refer you to the title of this book.)

She responded in kind. "NNNO!" She shouted.

"You don't tell me no." I said.

"NNNO!" She answered, and then charged toward me with her hand raised. When she reached my chair she swung, connecting with my forearm.

"What are you hitting me for?" I asked.

Her answer: "NNNO!"

Another slap.

My automatic reaction was to swat her butt. It was padded with a diaper and wasn't intended to hurt, but I hoped it was hard enough to startle her into realizing she needed to stop. Believe it or not she didn't get the message. A session of swapping licks ensued, until it became apparent that she wasn't going to give up. Finally I raised my voice to eleven, figuring that would surely do the trick, and it pissed her off even more. The ol' booming voice always worked wonders on my siblings and I when we were younger. Apparently I can't muster up the intensity and conviction that my dad always had. Abby fought back by biting my chair (wth?).

In the end I had to force her to sit against the wall, essentially putting her in the corner or, in terms that are a bit cringey to me though I don't know why, "time-out." The only problem was she didn't want to stay there. I had to stand about six inches from her. If I moved farther away she started scrambling like a running back through a defensive line, which drew me right back to her. At least twice I had to pick her up and, for lack of a better word, wrestle her into a sitting position. Eventually she tired of fighting me and gave in. There were tears. There was screaming. There was rage. Some of that was even from *her*.

And that, my friends, is why I find myself searching through online articles with titles like "How to Absolutely Love Parenting Your Toddler" or "How to Be a Calm, Cool, and Collected Parent"(Actual interesting reading, if you are so inclined).Two weeks ago I was marveling at how laid back my daughter was, and now I can't quite shake the feeling that I might be raising the next Hitler. Not the racist stuff, mind you, but I guarantee if you Sharpied a square on Abby's upper lip, slicked her hair over to the side, and slid a tiny podium in front of her she

would slap the hell out of that thing while shouting her
demands at her subjects - namely, my wife and I.

<u>Moral of the Story</u>: Take a breath. Count to three.

(Willy Wonka voice)
"Come with me,
and you'll be,
in a woooorld of toddler confrontation.

Keep it calm,
Grit your teeth,
Or you'll wind up in therapy..."

CHAPTER 25

The Molting

Things are weird.

Yesterday I looked out my front door and noticed the grass on my neighbor's lawn was a full inch shorter than mine. My jaw tightened. My eyes shrunk to slits. There was a slight quiver in the pockets of my cargo shorts as the anticipation rippled through the body that I've spent the last half decade cultivating into two hundred and thirty pounds of straight up dad meat.

That twang of irritation insisted on a simple solution. My grass could not be higher than my neighbor's.

In the garage there's a swoop of fabric as the cover is whipped from my Husqvarna. Its orange paint is coated in a layer of dust. Grass clippings rest atop the mowing deck. The hard plastic accents are freckled with grit and dried water spots. It needs detailing, but I'm not at that level yet. One step at a time.

After thirty minutes of mowing and another twenty of weed eating I stand on my porch and gaze across the green landscape. Now things are right. The playing field is even. Pun intended.

Over the past few years I've noticed certain changes taking place in my thought processes and decision making. There are even changes in my environment. For one, my shoes are turning white. Two years ago I was wearing black shoes. The next thing I know, my preference turned to gray and then, dear God, light gray. The path to glowing white shoes draws nigh.

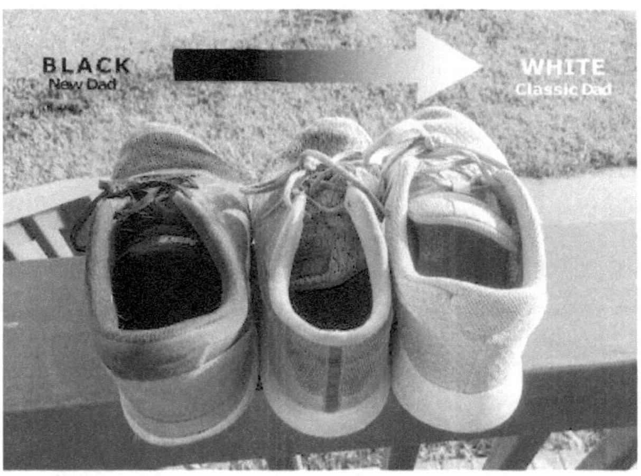

Another is that my biggest concern on our summer vacation is how to most efficiently deliver our supplies to our spot on the beach. I'm a pack mule. But that's just the tip of the iceberg.

There's more.

I can't grill without a beer. The thought of it disgusts me.

I'm comfortable wearing tank tops outside though I really, *really* shouldn't be.

I can physically feel it when a light is left on in an unoccupied room.

I find myself referring to my son as "buddy" or "big guy" more and more. "Tiger" and "sport" are just around the corner. I can feel it like a tickle in the back of my throat when I try to talk to him.

My legs are turning white. Like, bone white.

A few weeks ago I unknowingly bought a pair of shorts with an elastic waistband. They were cargo shorts. Columbia brand.

I've grown tolerant of country music. There are a handful of songs that I even *like*.

I already don't know where all my tools are, and my junk drawer is overflowing with things I haven't used in years but ones that I know I'll need again *someday*.

When I can't find a tool I stomp through the house, pissed off that "Nobody can ever find anything around here."

But this one, though, is the kicker. The other day my son showed me a picture of a deer in his new book, and as a reflex I immediately replied "Oh deer." He laughed! I've been slinging dad jokes since I met the kid, and he's finally to the age that he gets the jokes. These next few years are going to be awesome.

But still, the road to ultimate dadhood is a long one. Soon the jean shorts aisles will be calling to me in clothing stores. The tank tops will become too restrictive, and I'll need to lose them altogether. I will blossom out of them like a butterfly from a cocoon and when I do, I will instinctively know that I need to wash and wax the lawnmower after each use. I will know to complain about keeping the front door closed to save money on the energy bill. I will know to pull my hat over my eyes when in my recliner, and to tell my kids that "I'm not sleeping, I'm resting my eyes" or "I'm gonna stare at the back of my eyelids for a while."

Statements like "That's how they get you," "Let's get this show on the road," "Do you want me to give you something to cry about?" "They don't make 'em like they used to," "That's not going anywhere," and "Oh no, I think we'll have to amputate" are in the larval stages of growth somewhere in my mind. They're nudging against other requests like "You buying ours too?" when seeing coworkers at a restaurant during lunch, and the classic "Working hard or hardly working?" when passing someone in the office.

Inevitably there will come a time when a severe thunderstorm will roll through town. On that day, long after this phoenix has risen from the ashes of early fatherhood, while my family has already holed up in the storm shelter, I will step onto my front lawn and watch the clouds and rain move closer. I will stand tall and proud as if I could shield my family from the oncoming maelstrom with the strength of my World's Greatest Dad coffee mug, my collared shirt (painstakingly tucked into my khaki shorts), and my blinding white shoes with their accents of smeared lawn grass. Hopefully after an intense stare down I'll surrender to the storm and head in with my family. But you know, who really knows the true power of fatherhood? Could I take the storm?

CHAPTER 26

The Ties That Bind

I've forgotten a lot about what it feels like to be a kid, but one thing I do remember is how easy it is to be embarrassed in front of other kids. I also remember how you can hear someone say something, even if it's just an off-hand remark, and take it to heart without the speaker having any idea they've just rocked your world.

I screwed up the other day.

It all started two years ago, when Logan was four and my wife and I decided we'd get the jump on teaching him to tie his shoes. Logan's a smart kid, and we figured he'd take to it and have it figured out in an afternoon. A weekend, at most. We sat down with him, sat a shoe in his lap and went through the motions of tying one of his shoes while he followed along. I tried to show him the way I learned, and it went something like this:

> "Okay buddy, make an X with the strings. Now wrap the top one around the one on bottom, and pull both ends. No, not like that. That's not the top one, is it? There, that's the one. Loop it over the other one, tuck it back under, and pull."
>
> Logan pulls and the strings come apart; he sighs.
>
> "Nope. Try again."

He tries again and pulls the strings apart again. My blood pressure is like that stupid yodeler on the Price Is Right. The little bastard is climbing the mountain past ever increasing blood pressure values. 130/82.... 135/85... 141/90... 155/95. *Yodel-oh-ee-dee.* Logan tries again and barely gets the first part of the knot to work.

"Good! Good! See? This is easy, right? Now, make a loop."

He stares at me.

"Remember? Like this." I take the string and make a loop. "Now wrap the other string around the loop, but leave a little room at the bottom."

He stares at me. *Diddly-odel-oh-ee-dee...*165/98... 170/100... I do it for him.

"Okay now push the other string through the space at the the bottom, pull the loop through, and..."

He pulls the wrong string and it all unravels. He huffs. We repeat the process five or six more times with the same results. *Yodel-oh-ee-dee-ayee. Here comes the cliff edge.* 180/105... 185/108...

"I can't do it!" He yells.

The yodeler goes off the cliff.

It wasn't so much that he wasn't grasping the concept (which he wasn't), but that it was hard as hell to try and explain how to tie a knot to a four-year-old. Eventually Nikki and I - and Logan too, I think - got too frustrated and decided on the simple, kick-the-rock-down-the-road solution.

We bought him Velcro shoes.

Two years and two pairs of Velcro shoes later Logan was prepared to enter second grade and still didn't know how to tie his shoes. Enough was enough. Armed with the knowledge that this was going to be monumentally harder than we'd anticipated two years ago, we searched for some teaching aids. There is a video on Youtube that shows how to tie a shoe in an infinitely easier way than I had learned back in the mid-eighties (the video clip is titled "How To Tie a Shoe Step By Step" by Jennifer Hughes, for anyone interested). Nikki, Logan and I watched the video and he exclaimed "That's easy!" and asked for his shoe.

Hey, guess what? It wasn't easy. The video is extremely helpful - I'd recommend it to anyone - but seeing and doing are two different things. The strings of his new shoes were made of a material that does not lend itself to tightening easily into knots. It wasn't elastic enough, I think.

When we started I was patient. I probably deserved a medal for how calm and understanding I was in those first five minutes. I was certain we were about to have this problem solved. I watched Logan leaning over his shoe, carefully working the shoestrings one over the other, and every time he tried it would fall apart in front of his face.

"It's alright," I'd say, and each time Logan's breathing would get heavier as if he were revving up some internal engine. "Try again." I punctuated each mistake with statements like "Don't rush" and "It's okay you're doing fine."

The frustration began welling up in him as time after time the knot unraveled in his hands. Less than ten minutes in, Logan exploded.

"I can't do it!" He yelled.

"Yes you can. Try again."

Remember the yodeler from before? That guy was back, and he began his ascent of Mount Blood Pressure.

I guided Logan as best I could. Eventually after a lot of anger and frustration, things began to turn around. He made the first part, the pretzel, flawlessly. He got to the second pretzel, made it, and prepared for step three, the loops. The loops always foiled him. His fingers grabbed the loops, pulled outward, and the strings slipped like limp noodles out of the knot.

Logan growled. Seriously, growled like a wolf. "I can't do it!" He yelled again, and the tears came.

Yodel-oh-ee-dee.

"I know you can do it." I went through the whole diatribe about how smart he was and how easy this would seem once he gets it right.

Logan wasn't buying it. He clammed up with his arms folded. I was agitated myself, in part because now he was so mad he was trying to mess it up. I was more mad though because I couldn't really tell him what he was doing wrong. My agitation grew as his did.

And then I screwed up.

Out of my own frustration I said "Do you want to be the only kid in second grade who can't tie his shoes? Do you want to be made fun of?"

It just popped out. I didn't think he'd even heard it, to be honest. I figured he was so mad he wasn't hearing anything.

Two days later we were getting ready for work and school and Logan was still struggling with his shoes. I heard him lose his temper and then I heard crying. I walked into the kitchen where Logan sat on the floor with his shoes untied.

"What's wrong?" I asked, knowing damn well what was wrong.

Nikki walked up to me and, out of earshot of Logan, said "He's afraid the kids will make fun of him because he still can't do it."

It hit home.

At that point I became the Incredible Shrinking Man. The Hubble telescope wouldn't have been able to see me if it had been hovering outside my own front door, I felt so small.

I couldn't stop thinking about Logan that day. I thought about what it was like to be a kid. I remembered feeling confused a lot. Not intelligent enough, not fast enough or tall enough or thin enough or whatever other "enough" that people try to use to measure a person's worth. If I recall correctly I was one of the last in my class to learn how to tie shoes. I don't know why my mind held onto this, but I remember holding a paper cutout of a shoe with holes punched in it, and laces looped through the holes like a real shoe. We were supposed to tie them in class, and I had to whisper to a friend to help me because I couldn't do it.

When you're a kid you're still trying to find your place in the world. A lot of it doesn't make sense (hell, it still doesn't as an adult) and sometimes it's scary or uncomfortable or lonely or confusing. To this day I sometimes have this suspicion that everyone but me is in on some sort of understanding about life that I'm not privy to. Maybe we all think that, though, and some people are just really good at hiding it. Or maybe that suspicion comes from my own inadequacies, perceived or actual. I'm not sure but I can say this, though. However frustrated I get, I will never again suggest that fear of shame or embarrassment is a good motivator to learn how to do something. It's hard enough to get along in the world without having to worry whether or not you measure up to someone else's idea of what you should be.

Well that got deep, didn't it? Sort of like a closing monologue on an episode of *The Wonder Years*. Read it in a Daniel Stern voice, if you don't mind.

<u>Moral of the Story:</u>

1) Kids hear what you say more than you think they do.
2) Self esteem is more important than aptitude. There is a quote usually attributed to Albert Einstein that says that everyone is a genius, but if you judge a fish by his ability to climb a tree, he'll live his whole life believing he's a failure. Whether Einstein said it or not, it's something to think about.

Read that in a Daniel Stern voice too. In fact, read all these posts in a Daniel Stern voice. Those vocal chords are a national treasure.

CHAPTER 27

The Slow-Down Period

My brother and I are sitting outside on his patio furniture. One of his teen daughters sits across from us, not paying us any attention. The other is in town with her new boyfriend. We turn our attention to my daughter, just two years old and crawling around on the outdoor sofa beside her cousin.

"It goes by so fast." My brother says, and there's a bitterness in the way he says it. There's passion and sincerity too, but more than anything else there's a palpable sense of longing.

How many times had I heard a parent say that over the years? How many times had I (at least inwardly) rolled my eyes at the thought, shrugged it off as something adults say to pass the time like talking about the weather?

Now a father myself, I know exactly what that statement means. It's a warning. It's an attempt to alert us new parents that this won't last forever, that you need to hold tight to your kids now and treasure every moment - even the frustrating ones - because it will one day be gone and you'll be begging for it back again.

It's also, I think, a plea. It's begging time to slow for just a little while, maybe give us a rewind button so we can hold our kids again after they've grown too large for such things. It's the thought that maybe, just maybe if we say it enough, somehow we will be transported back to a time before the world drew them away from us, a time when we were everything to them.

When we were most important.

The irony is that as a parent of two young children, I already know this. I know it and despite that knowledge I let the time pass by anyway. I get tired of their energy, I get bored with the things they want to watch on TV (darn you Blippi), I want to scroll on Facebook or work on some stupid blog (hehe) in my spare time instead of watch Logan furiously clack two action figures together as they "fight" or listen to "Wheels on the Bus" for the three-hundredth time with Abby.

Labor Day Weekend: I spent most of the long weekend hanging out with Nikki and Abby. Logan was at his dad's for the weekend. We had Abby's 2nd birthday party, which Logan did attend. We didn't do much otherwise, mostly sat on the bed and watched Abby's little sing-along videos on Youtube, and walked in the park a couple of times. An unproductive weekend, really. But, as I handed my daughter over to her mom Tuesday morning, as I watched her little face bouncing to the cadence of Nikki's footsteps while being carried toward the car, that feeling hit. Most parents know the one. A heavy, sinking feeling. Longing. Knowing that time is perpetually changing, always moving forward, and all we can do is smile and wave as it walks out the door. I found myself hearing, of all things, a country song that gets me every time I hear it (despite the fact that it's corny as hell and I would have laughed it off the radio when I was younger, before I had kids) called "It Won't Be Like This For Long."

I remember a story my mother told me about when my oldest brother started school. I'm probably going to mangle this a little bit, but it went something like this: She dropped my brother off that first day and watched him walk up the steps to the door. When he got to the door he turned and looked at her for a few seconds, and then walked inside. I don't know if my mom had a job at that time, but I have to assume she spent the majority of the first years of my brother's life at his side. Then one day she had to turn him over to school. When they looked at each other that morning they must have both known that this was the end of an era, that things were moving on.

The reason I remember her telling this story is because she went with him when he moved into a dorm in college some twelve years later. She sat in her car and watched him walk toward the building (I'm assuming the dormitory), and just before he went in he turned and looked at her just like he'd done on that first day of school. They waved at each other as the car pulled away. The end of another era. That brought all the memories flooding back to her, and I imagine the dam broke then.

And now my brother is in her shoes, watching his oldest working a job and going to college, while his youngest is inching towards graduation from high school next year. I guess one day if all goes as planned I'll be doing the same when my time comes. By my calculations I have eleven years before that day for Logan and sixteen years for Abby. The circle keeps turning. I believe there's a song on *The Lion King* that says something about this whole mess.

When you're a parent the majority of your life revolves around your kids. Most of the time it feels like you're running a losing race, trying to get too much done in too little time. You get home from eight hours of work to discover your kid has homework and they need your help. Homework, dinner, baths, and by then it's bedtime. Repeat the cycle tomorrow. And the next day. When you get a few days extra, like a Labor Day weekend, the race stops for a bit. You get a slow-down period. You can take a few breaths and actually spend time with your family without succumbing to the routine you know is waiting on idle just around the bend.

That's why I had the sinking feeling the morning after Labor Day, I think. I had an extra day of quality time with Abby. In those times I get to marvel at the person my daughter is becoming. I get to hear her talk with an ever expanding vocabulary that surprises me every day. I get to watch her explore and learn. I get to see her growing before my very eyes, and because of that time sort of slows down, if only for a few moments. It's only time enough for me to recognize that it's happening. Then it's back to work and school, back on the tracks we've constructed that carry us efficiently through our weekday lives. When Nikki and Abby left that morning they carried the slow-down period with them, and now its back to the races. Until the next one I'll only catch glimpses of how quickly she and Logan are growing, how smart they're becoming, how they're turning into little *people*. I'm already ready for the next slow down.

<u>Moral of the Story:</u> I guess it's obvious. Take note of the extra time with the kids. Cling to it, immerse yourself in it, squeeze it tight even though it'll slip through your fingers anyway. In the end you'll still be saying "It goes by too fast," but every bit of slow-down helps.

Look at me, being all philosophical.

CHAPTER 28

Hey Jerk, Get Off Your Phone!

I don't usually consider myself a millennial even though I think I technically fall into that category, at least by some estimations. I was born in '81 and was privileged to be part of the generation that sort of got the best of both worlds, as far as kids' interests go. I'm old enough to have spent the majority of my childhood days outside playing with sticks and pine cones, exploring the woods, and riding my bike all over the place, but my later childhood also saw a boom in technology. Namely, video games and VCR's. As I got older and technology continued to grow, I was part of the generation that first began to carry cell phones (albeit it was the size of a small brick, with a six inch retractable antenna, and came with a stern warning from my mother of "Do not use unless it's an emergency, each minute costs money.").

Cell phones advanced, and I was in my early twenties when text messaging exploded. You could text all you wanted, too! As long as the person you were texting was using the same phone service, that was. Otherwise you had to wait until after nine o'clock for free texting.

Unlimited nights and weekends!

Basically I became a young adult right as the flashy cell phones with all the little bells and whistles were being marketed towards people in my demographic. Soon came smart phones and social media, Youtube, and all the rest. No longer would I have to sit bored in a waiting room. No longer would I be bored waiting for anything, really, as long as I had that phone. Untold thousands (or millions?) of apps were available, giving me endless ways to amuse myself in my down time. I could read books on my phone. I could play games, use a calculator, talk to friends, shop online, listen to music, look up which actor played in what movie, learn about the Cuban Missile Crisis if I wanted. The possibilities were endless.

How easy it is to get addicted to something like that. Today a cell phone for most people is pretty much a part of their wardrobe. I'd no sooner forget mine than I would my car keys. What if I need to get in touch with someone? What if my car breaks down or I have a flat tire? What if the school needs to get in touch with me about one of the kids? What am I going to look at while sitting at lunch? If I'm sitting on my bed at night, it's beside me or in my hands. My hands reflexively reach for it whenever I sit still for too long, or if I feel the slightest bit bored.

The glaring, obvious problem with all of this is that it draws you away from the present. You spend your time staring at that glowing rectangle instead of interacting with the people around you. My son, God love him, called me

out on this in the most subtle yet effective way just the
other day.

Earlier that night he'd made a plan. I was supposed to go
with him to his room when it was time for Abby to go to
bed. We were going to hang out in there for fifteen
minutes before it was his bedtime.
We were all sitting on the bed in our master bedroom, and
the time came. Logan stood up.

"Let's go," he said.

I stood and immediately reached for my phone.
Logan saw this and murmured under his breath, "Why do
you always have to bring that?"

I think he said it mostly to himself, more of a frustrated
statement than a question meant for me. I slid the phone in
my pocket, and as it dropped heavily and bumped the side
of my leg, a matching thud of guilt hit home inside. Why
was I bringing my phone? What purpose would it serve if
the fifteen minutes Logan was requesting was meant for
bro time? The more I thought about it, the more I realized
grabbing my phone was a dick move.

To my credit the phone stayed in my pocket during our
hangout time that night. That's not always the case,
though, even now. The phone creeps back in. There's a
horror movie idea in here somewhere, I just know it. Some
half-sentient phone that longs to be human, and it's got
some creepy fetish about always wanting to be cradled in a
human palm. Keeps finding ways to subtly crawl back into
your hand.
Okay so it's a B-movie.

<u>Moral of the Story:</u> If your kids are annoying you while
you look on your phone, there's a good chance that you are

the annoying one. Put the phone down, ya jerk! Cell phones are fun but at the end of the day they're a tool and nothing more. They aren't friends or family, and can never take the place of them. Even if they are soul-starved, half-alive beings intent on taking over humanity, or creepy little robot kinksters that just want to be held all day.

CHAPTER 29

Ingenuity

The laws of physics can be cruel.

I can't dunk a basketball. I can't fly, I can't camouflage myself to blend in with my environment, I can't burn holes through concrete with my laser eyesight. I don't have a single, solitary superpower that I'm aware of (unless you count the ability to smile and nod as if I understand a topic while in a conversation even though my mind is doing cartwheels in the land of make-believe).

I have, however, developed a decent understanding of the basic laws of physics over the almost forty years I've roamed this earth. On occasion I use that knowledge to my advantage, and harness its power for the forces of good.

Case in point: Abby and I were in the Dairy Queen drive thru after I'd picked her up from daycare a couple of weeks ago. There are a few toys I have in my car to keep the kids entertained when they ride with me. One is a stuffed Godzilla and the other is a tiny football that fits in the palm of your hand. Abby chose the football as the source of entertainment for the ride home, and that did not bode well for me. Godzilla, destructive as he is, can pass for what Logan would call a "snuggly toy." It's just something soft to hold against you. Abby holds him and plays with him within the confines of her car seat.

The football is a different story. There is enough college football playing at our house (whenever it's on she points at the screen and yells "Foopah!") for our daughter to understand at least the most basic actions required by the sport.

She knows to throw the ball.

This inevitably leads to a high pitched shriek the minute it leaves her hand. Being strapped into a car seat like a Talladega racecar driver doesn't allow for much of a reach. She throws it, immediately realizes she wants it back but can't reach it, and at least eighty percent of the time I can't get to it myself to hand it back to her. I get to drive the rest of the way home to the song of a mad, whiny toddler.

That night I had made it all the way from town to the Dairy Queen near home without issue. After I'd placed the order with the young lady, I crept forward toward the window to get our food.

Abby let out a whine.

"What's wrong?" I asked in my playful, counter-whine voice.

"Foopah!" Abby responded.

I turn and see the little ball nestled above the middle seat beneath the rear window. It had landed in the perfect location to torment both myself and my daughter. It was within eyesight of her, but just out of reach. With my seatbelt on I couldn't reach it either, and as soon as I tried the car in front of me moved forward and I had to follow the train of vehicles.

"I wan' my foopah!" Abby called.

"I can't reach it, honey. You're gonna have to wait a minute."

Good thing my daughter is extremely patient, right? Wrong.

"I WAN' MY FOOPAH!"

I try to reach for it again. No dice. By that time I had gotten to the window and had handed the girl my debit card. An unreasonable yet determined wave of anxiety washed over me. I didn't have time to unbuckle. The minute I did and worked around to a kneeling position in the driver's seat (assuming I could even *achieve* this without causing a scene with my ass bumping into the horn on the steering wheel or something) she'd be back to hand me my card and my food. She'd have to watch me awkwardly shift and struggle while the car shook with my efforts and my daughter screamed for her foopah in the background. I wasn't having it.

"I can't reach it yet Abby." Used her actual name that time. Hopefully that would let her know I meant business.

"I.. WAN'... MY FOOPAH..." The tears began.

Anxiety and frustration buzzed like the whine of a half dozen mosquitos hovering just outside my ear.
The worker handed me the food and the debit card. I took a quick glance at the rearview mirror and noted there was only one other car behind me, and they were still placing their order. My focus changed to the little red ball taunting me at the edge of the seat. Abby's hand reached out for it periodically.

And that's when I knew what I had to do.

It's funny how stress forces answers into your brain. Maybe they aren't the smartest answers, but when you're back's against the wall your brain starts pulling from any available experience or bit of half-baked intelligence you might possess. You start calculating, running risk analyses, taking complete stock of your surroundings and making decisions in rapid fire succession.

I was not going to listen to my daughter whining for the rest of the ride home.

My idea was a simple one. I crept the car forward until I was out of the way of the drive thru window. I looked left, I looked right. Satisfied, I nodded to myself.

I stepped on the gas, the force of acceleration pushing me back against my seat for a second or two, and then I immediately hit the brakes.

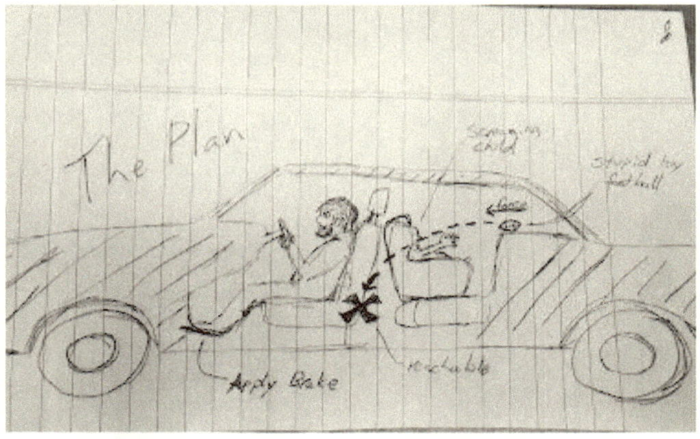

The change in force pushed me forward. Abby, strapped firmly into her car seat, probably felt nothing. The football shot forward and hit the back of the console near my elbow with a satisfying thud. I reached back, grabbed the ball that was now easily within reach, and handed it to my fussing daughter.

I reveled in my victory for a moment, thinking of how ingenious the solution had been. I held a half smile on my face for roughly the next minute and a half...

Until she threw the damn ball again.

<u>Moral of the Story</u>: I don't know. Just don't give your kid something that they feel inspired to throw when on trips in the car. You won't always be able to harness the power of physics to help.

CHAPTER 30

And All Through The House…

There's a little ritual that my wife and I both take part in. Maybe it's a rite of passage for parents, or a necessary obstacle to try and salvage your sanity in the face of nonstop loud noises, voices, fights, and run-stomping that sounds like a herd of bison tearing through your home and not just two young kids playing. I practice this ritual on the weekend mornings, and my wife does it while Abby naps during midday.

(Cue the Mission Impossible music)

I swing my feet over the side of the bed and let them sink slowly into the carpet. The first test presents itself. Will the floorboards creak? Doesn't matter, it's a chance I have to take. I stand, putting my full weight on my two feet, and hear only the faintest of sounds of protest from the floor.
Good.

Using the balls of my feet - and my toes for balance - I creep toward the bedroom door. Daylight is already beginning to filter into the room from the window, and my watch reads six-thirty a.m. I have time. Surely I have time.

The hallway presents the biggest challenge. In days past I'd sneak right down the center of the hall, hearing floorboards protest in sounds ranging from short, dry murmurs to shrieks of dumb fury at every other step. Only a few months ago did my wife let me in on a little secret: if you stay near the walls the floor is less likely to creak.

So that's what I do. I hug the wall like a jumper on a ledge who's had second thoughts. My feet shuffle against the baseboards. The farther I get away from the door at the end of the hall, the more carefree I can be, but it's best not to chance it. Right now it's 6:32 and I have a good fifteen or twenty minutes to myself. Maybe even thirty. Who knows? A man can dream, right?

The call of nature is usually strong in the morning. Luckily a bathroom rests halfway down the hall, on the opposite side of bedrooms. If you're a guy, you're in luck. You can aim. The trick is to not hit the actual water with your stream, or it'll sound like a mini waterfall inside the house. You skirt the water in the toilet, aim for the sides of the bowl. This method will almost eliminate sound altogether from your morning bathroom routine. With that deed done I wash my hands (using the low setting for the sink faucet, allowing only a murmur of water instead of a high pressure blast), and it's time to continue the trek to the ultimate destination: the recliner in the living room. There's only one more stop to make.

I make it into the kitchen. Here, there are two loud sounds that could spell doom for my brief time of solitude.

One is the hot water knob at the kitchen sink. For some reason, the knob for hot water lets out its own screech every time you turn it. I'm a lefty and no matter how hard I try to remember to just turn the damn cold water knob with my right hand instead, ol' Mr. Left has a mind of its own and reaches for the closest one before I can stop it.

Why do I have to turn the water on at all, though, right?

Coffee is why. Without that hot, sweet bean nectar this time alone will mean nothing. It'll be spent trying to clear my head and focus my eyes while a random song plays on repeat in my head (seriously, every morning of my life that I can remember has been accompanied by a soundtrack. Sometimes it's a good one, more often I'm getting Rick-rolled or hearing Baby Shark on a loop). Without coffee I'll sit on the recliner and wonder what day it is until I hear Abby start calling my name. So I have to have coffee. Hence, I have to turn on the water to fill the pot.

That brings us to the second loud sound: the coffee maker itself. Granted, it's not too loud, but it still coughs and burps little exclamations of noise into an otherwise quiet house. Add to that my (hopefully dainty) footsteps tip-toeing back and forth to and from the pot, it can be the recipe for disaster.

I lived alone for several years before I got married. I'm introverted, and alone time was my jam. I like being around people, sure, but I always enjoyed going home and sitting in the silence of my house, watching a movie or playing a video game or reading.

Now, roughly ten years later, I'm experiencing the flip side of that coin. I wouldn't trade my married life with my kids for anything, but it does not offer an ample amount of time to oneself. I can give up my alone time, but I'm still going to scrounge for little pockets of it whenever I can get it like a druggy jonesing for his next fix.

So I do my little covert waltz through the house. I tip-toe, I wince when my weight causes a snap, crackle or pop, I breathe shallow and slowly ease myself into my recliner. Well over half the time I realize once I've sat down, and once the faux leather has stopped squawking, that I have forgotten the book I was going to read or that my phone is laying on the kitchen island. It requires extra sound to make up for that error. A good rule to remember: Always picture yourself in your spot of rest, doing what you plan to do. What all is around you? What do you need to bring?

In the end my sneaking usually doesn't pan out. Not for any useful length of time, anyway. I may make it a page or two into a book, but inevitably a little voice in the back of the house speaks up.

"Daddy?"

And if you don't answer? If you think, *maybe she's still half asleep. Maybe she'll drift off for a few more minutes*? Well then the voice gets more assertive.

"Daddy." (No longer a question. A statement, short-clipped, bordering on admonishment.)

"Daddy, tum dit me." (Translates into "Daddy, come get me.")

And if I wait too much longer the little voice begins to wail. "I wan' dit outta dis!"

If that voice doesn't speak up first, there's another sound. I'll hear a door open in the hall. A seven-year-old whirlwind will zip toward me, ready to play immediately and fully prepared to send me on a guilt trip if I say no.

And it's all okay. It's great, even. Alone time can play second fiddle to the boy that spins through the house like the Tasmanian devil or the little smiling girl that calls from the back room. I imagine I'll get my alone time back in some form years from now, and I doubt I'll be looking forward to it so much by then.

Even knowing all that I still sneak alone time when I can get it. Tomorrow I know I'll be back to hugging the wall and slinking my way through the house, avoiding creaky floors and working the coffee pot as if it were a dangerous chemistry experiment, hissing to myself at any noise I make, praying for just a few minutes of solitude before the sounds begin.

Moral of the Story: Alone time is great. I mean GREAT. But not as great as spending these younger years with the kids that are literally begging you to notice them at all times. If they interrupt your alone time, give them a pass. Every time. That's what I keep telling myself, anyway.

CHAPTER 31

Where is Abby?

Fun fact about me: My attention span can be measured by microscope. You know how you can look forever for your sunglasses and find out after ten minutes of rummaging through your house that they were pulled up on your head the whole time? I've got that beat.

A few weeks ago in a land not so far away...

It was a fine spring day, warm in the sun but cool in the shade, a deep blue sky overhead carrying a fleet of clouds so white they almost glowed. The kids had soccer games. (Well, "game" might be a stretch for what Abby and her age group are doing. It's more of a boot camp for toddlers. Imagine disturbing an ant hill and then trying to teach each ant how to dribble a soccer ball with the inside edge of their feet, or dodge plastic cones by dribbling around them in a maze, or hop through rings laid out in a specific pattern. That is a toddler "game" of soccer). Before the games, though, the kids were supposed to get their pictures made. It was a frenzy of attempted order that resulted in chaos. Children were scattered across the fields, revolving in ever-widening circles around their parents and trying to break free of their folks' gravitational pull. The parents themselves walked around confused, unsure of which line to stand in. Random kids shouted or cried or laughed.

As we entered the park I could see several sub-lines that had formed in front of a row of soccer goals. The photographers had set up here. Kids and parents alike were being ushered (herded) through the lines with calm yet firm haste towards the photo lines. Those lines were the end goal, but before that we learned we had to stand in the first line, a big fat snake of a thing that crossed the main walkway from the concession stand and curved into the fields where the cameras awaited.

My wife, who is the force of order and organization in our family, stood silently losing her mind in the chaos from the minute we arrived. Being the force of absent-minded lollygagging, I just stood there watching it all, waiting for our turn. The depths of my (probably diagnosable) ADD are almost boundless, and today those depths sunk even deeper into the abyss.

Observe the aging gray-headed southeastern moron as he interacts in the wild:

As we stood in line Abby played with another kid on her "team." At one point she took a spill and landed on her butt. She started crying so I picked her up and held her. Several minutes went by, in which Logan tested boundaries by wandering farther and farther from us. With all the commotion going on I couldn't focus on any one thing for more than a few seconds. My brain was playing ping pong with my vision. The problem was, my eyes were faster than my brain.

It all happened in less than two seconds.

For one fleeting moment of moronitude (new word; you're welcome), a synapse snapped in my mind. I couldn't see my daughter anywhere! Panic sputtered like a candle flame in my stomach and I said aloud for everyone to hear, "Where's Abby?" I even turned to scan the throng of people. She'd wandered out of my field of vision, I was sure. That's when I noticed the weight in my arm.

I was holding her.

When my head spun to locate her I found myself face to face with her blue eyes.

"What did you say?" Nikki asked from beside me.

I chuckled. "I said Abby, but I meant Logan. Where's Logan?"

Here's a little secret, though: I didn't mean Logan. Yes, I really did forget for a second that I was holding my own daughter and started to look for her. Yes, for approximately one and a half seconds my brain farted so hard I felt its wind ruffle my hair. Yes, daydreaming all day is probably bad and all those years being absent minded have caught up with me in my old age.

I'm going to be forty in a few months. I thought my body might at least give me those few months before it started its slow crumble.

I was wrong.

Moral of the Story: Exercise your mind. Sharpen your focus. Read books, play memory games, be aware of things, don't get old. Most of that's easy to do.
Or so you would think.

CHAPTER 32

It's All In The Reflexes

Well it's soccer season again. Time for us parents to sit in our fold-out chairs and eat popcorn or chips and pretend like we know what we're talking about when we call out to our kids on the field. Time for us to yell things at them like "Just kick the ball!" or "Pay attention here it comes!" or "Wrong goal! Wrong goal!" in an attempt to confuse them as much as possible.

Okay, that's not the intention but I'll be damned if it doesn't happen every game. In truth, though, Logan is finally learning the fundamentals. He's eight years old and has played since he was four, and you can see the wheels turning when he plays now. He's scored a few times, he hustles more, he knows how to pass and what the difference is between offense and defense. He plays with a little confidence now. He and his age group have also gotten pretty good at kicking the ball, too.

Kicking it hard.

Which is where my fatherly instincts come in. I sit in my red folding throne like an emperor watching a battle in the colosseum. I nod approvingly when my team scores. I say things like "They're not getting back on defense fast enough," or "They've got to shoot before they get too close to the goal or the goalie will pick it up every time." followed by, ten seconds later, "See? Every time..." (for more on my soccer knowledge credentials, see footnote #1)

I'm already flexing some dad muscles here. Specifically the one I like to call The Commentator, wherein from the comfort of my chair I not only understand the fundamentals and the strategics of the game I'm watching, I magically know how to impart that knowledge onto a player from the far sidelines by barking commands to a kid who in all likelihood can't even hear me. It's quite a skill to have.

So I'm lounging there, analyzing the game while my white knees are burning in the brutal Autumn sun, when the capacity for my dad powers are tested. A soccer ball flies toward us, courtesy of an errant kick (kid probably kicked with his toes and not the side of his foot, but that's beside the point). It bounces once but shows no sign of slowing down.

My daughter is standing in the ball's path.

I have maybe two seconds. Without even leaving my lounge chair, I lean forward and kick my leg out in front of my daughter like a traffic barricade arm in a parking deck. I have a split second to gauge the height of the ball. I shift my leg up a couple of centimeters.

The wind brushes the hairs on my legs. It's a southeasterly. I adjust for windage.

At the last second the ball strikes my calf a few inches above my sandal and bounces harmlessly away. A chorus of nearby parents praise my heroism. I smile and nod, wave at a couple of them. "Dad reflexes," I reply. "Just the dad reflexes." (see footnote 2. Or just ignore it. No need to read it really. LET ME HAVE THIS!)

After all the ooh's and aaah's we settle back down in our chairs. I bask in the reverence for only an instant. The boys have played on, and I return my attention to the field. With my daughter sitting safely beside me, it seems I still have a soccer game to analyze….

Moral of the Story: Know your surroundings. Be vigilant. You never know when your child will need you to instantly transfer dad powers from The Commentator to The Bodyguard in the blink of an eye.

Oh, and second moral: Don't read footnotes.

Footnote #1: I've never played a game of soccer in my life, except for on a school playground.

Footnote #2: Okay, so the ball wasn't really going that fast. If anything it would have glanced off my daughter's chest and maybe caused her to take a step back. She'd whine for about five seconds and she'd be fine. And really it wasn't like I reacted with the speed of a striking snake. In fact I'm fairly certain I grunted when I lifted my leg up to block it.

CHAPTER 33

I Wish I Was A Baller

Well getting older sucks.

I'll explain. Logan has started playing basketball. This is his second season playing, really, but the first season playing for Sacred Heart, his school's team. It's the same school team I played for back in the 1900's when I was a kid, and the fact that he's on that team and will be playing on that court where my little L.A. Gear sneakers had once tread has brought with it a feeling of nostalgia for me. I'm not exactly an athlete, but I was decent at basketball. I was never aggressive enough, but I could shoot and dribble with the best of them.

Last weekend I had the kids to myself for a couple of hours, and I decided to take them to the park in town. It was a nice, clear day, if a little chilly with a breeze. Logan's dad (I'm his stepdad, for those who don't know) is coach of his basketball team and had asked him to practice his dribbling, so we took our well-worn basketball with us to the park to practice.

Abby decided to take her toy soccer ball. We walked along, with Logan awkwardly dribbling down the path, until we made it to the outdoor court that had recently been renovated. It's a full sized concrete court with fresh blue paint in the keys. Logan took to shooting immediately, and I was for the moment preoccupied with making sure Abby didn't wander too far away on the soccer fields surrounding the court. Once I made sure she was good, running around in the field beside us, I turned my attention to Logan.

"Feed me the rock." I said and held out my hands. I'm sure he had no idea what that expression meant (hello 90's slang!) but he eventually understood that I wanted the ball. He tossed it to me.

Watch this, I thought, and edged backward until I was behind the three-point line.

I shot the ball.

It whooshed through the air. My aim was on. I could see it travelling straight toward the goal, and almost nodded to myself before I saw it fall about five feet short of even grazing the rim. I frowned. Logan chased after it.

"Give me another one." I called to him after he'd trotted back from the field that the ball had bounced into. He tossed it to me again. I squared up. Took the shot.

Airball.

The wind, I thought, *the wind is knocking it down.*

"Again," I called to Logan, and he bounced it to me. I fired, this time using pretty much all of my arm strength, feeling like I was shooting a half court shot.

Airball.

Well this is bullshit, I thought. Thankfully I didn't say that out loud. I always prided myself on my shooting ability. That was the thing I could do. I'd gone to the county free throw competition because of my knack for shooting accuracy. I was put into games sometimes solely to shoot free throws when a technical foul was called. And now I can't even hit the bottom of the net from the three-point line with a youth basketball. My how the mighty have fallen.

I turned forty a few months ago. When I do the math, I realize it's been at the very least ten years since I've played any sort of basketball, save for shooting on the kiddie goal at home that even I, with my 2.3 inch vertical leap, can dunk on. I'd venture to say in reality it's been more than fifteen years since I've really played. I guess your body can only remember how to do it for so long before it just gives up.

My Muscle Memory: "Yeah, this dude's forty years old. He's never gonna play basketball again. No point in remembering this garbage."

I shot about ten more three-pointers that afternoon, and only rung one of them. The others were mostly airballs. I found myself hoping to just hit the rim, for crying out loud. I think it's safe to say Logan didn't walk off the court that day thinking "Wow, he's a great basketball player." He didn't follow behind me as I strutted away, wishing he could shoot like me.

On the upside, though, Logan's shooting and dribbling has gotten infinitely better since last year. Most of what I did that day was let him dribble and shoot while I nursed my bruised ego, and he played well! I guess I'm going to need to sneak out to the courts and practice by myself a little, or he'll be beating me in one-on-one by the time he's ten years old.

And I can't let that happen.

Moral of the Story: Before you try and show your kid how good you are at something, best make sure you are actually good at it.

CHAPTER 34

Whirlwind

My mind is sometimes a whirlwind. Ideas and thoughts and goals are pieces of debris that get kicked up and scattered in the spiral until the wind dies down and they're thrown toward every point on the compass. In the tumult, thoughts are easily lost or misplaced. I blame my age, for one. For another, I blame the technology driven, social media info orgy we're all drowning in. Or maybe I should just blame myself for submitting to it all (though I kinda have to submit to age, right? The passage of time? Is there a way around that one? Hmmm. That's a pickle.)

I'm always on the lookout to combat this scatterbrained lifestyle, and just recently I stumbled across a book about something called bullet journaling. It's a way to organize your day to day thoughts, ideas, tasks and experiences. It's supposed to make you re-evaluate how you spend your time. It's supposed to harness all those random thoughts floating around in your head and aim them towards whatever goal you want to achieve.

Last night I laid down after putting Abby to bed. My wife sat beside me, working on her computer. I was setting up my first bullet journal, and as a true adult who enjoys getting a nice pair of comfortable socks and a new belt for

Christmas, preparing this journal was exciting. I could see it coming together.

"Daddy!"

Abby's voice rings throughout the house, courtesy of the baby monitor with the volume on high. I laid there quietly, like an idiot, hoping she wouldn't call out again.

"Daddy!" She called.

I knew this was coming. We've reached the stage where she "has to potty" every night after being tucked in to bed.

I roll out of bed. As I make my way into the hall she calls "I need to go potty!"

I lift her from the crib and carry her into the bedroom, and then let her down when we reach the master bathroom. I step aside while she does her business (this time she actually did go, but there's always a good chance she's just bullshitting). When she's done I carry her back to bed, where she insists that I first pat her back and then rub her arm before I'm allowed to leave.

My chores done, I stand up and leave.

I flop down on the bed, re-open my journal, and continue to set it up.

"Oh no," Abby says to herself, just loud enough to hear it on the monitor. "Daddy!" She calls.

"What?" I call back.

"We forgot to put my medicine on my chest."

The damn Vapo-rub. Another ploy to get me to come back in. Nikki had put it on her chest about a week ago when she'd had the sniffles, and she's insisted on it every night since.

Before all this it was the tablet. We'd broken unspoken parental law and let Abby lie in bed for about fifteen minutes with a tablet to watch her Steve and Maggie videos. Nikki put a timer on it, and it didn't take long for Abby to figure out she could push the little button on the side and turn it back on after it had gone dead. So thirty minutes went by and Nikki and I had looked at each other and then back at the monitor where the tablet was clearly illuminating our daughter's face, and we understood the folly of our ways. I'd gone into her room then (for the first time this night) and when I took the tablet I asked why it was still on.

"I pushed the little button because I wanted to keep watching," she answered simply.

That was trip number one to Abby's room. Potty came second. Vapo-Rub came third. Each time I clambered out of bed with nary a single word written in the bullet journal, and my plans for organizing my thoughts were thwarted by a three-year-old that didn't want to go to sleep. I even tried to get her to count sheep, a tactic that has probably never truly worked in the history of ever.

I apply the Vapo-Rub, and politely threaten her that I will not be coming back into this room again. She whines. We argue. Eventually I talk her into lying down and I walk out.

Falling back onto bed, I resume setting up my bullet journal. I'm happy to say that I did get it completely set up, eventually, and Abby finally relented for the night and fell asleep.

My night trying to get my daughter to go to bed is sort of a microcosm of parenting in general. The moral of this story, I suppose, is that time is precious. When children are involved, time and focus become the rarest of commodities, and, by law, cannot exceed the limit of five minute time intervals. Snatch it when you can.

EPILOGUE

As I sit writing this, my wife is packing up clothes and posting things on Facebook for sale. We're moving. Cardboard boxes are beginning to populate each room. I'm listening to my Chill 2021 playlist on Spotify, which consists of the likes of "She Talks To Angels" by The Black Crowes, "The Flame" by Cheap Trick, "Disarm" and "1979" by The Smashing Pumpkins, and a few dozen more. I wonder vaguely if my kids will hear this music the same way I'd have heard Credence Clearwater Revival, The Beatles, or The Oak Ridge Boys back when I was a kid, when my dad would play them on record or cassette tape. My wife has said "Dear God I can't believe how many movies we have" like seven times. No lie. I stand over those boxes of movies with my fists on my hips and a proud smile on my face, and I think that pisses her off even more. Gotta have fun where you can, boys.

I've always had trouble accepting change. Each time I've moved to a new house, or left a job or a school I'd attended, I've felt varying degrees of that same pang that hits at the intersection between memory and love. Each time I've taken a look back and let memories wash through until they sank deep inside, and as I pull the door closed it all felt like slow motion. This is it, I'll think. The end of an era. Things are different, forever.

I gotta tell you, kids make that shit worse. As I walk through our current house I see the spots where I first saw our daughter walk. I think of the walker she'd use to chase me down the hallway, one that sounded like a dozen tiny bowling balls rolling down the lane all at once. I remember turning around with outstretched zombie arms and chasing her back down the hall, to the tune of her laughter. I'll see the front yard and remember Logan and I wrestling in the grass or playing soccer. I'll think of watching Godzilla movies on a bro's night with Logan. I'll remember sitting in my recliner holding Abby and reading *Dance, Dance, Baby*, her favorite book. I'll remember my wife and I sitting in our lawn chairs at night after the kids went to bed, counting satellites, sometimes even having a little to drink, while the sounds in the neighborhood died down and the stars winked above us like a sea of blue candle flames. There will be a part of me that wants to just stand in that house forever, knowing all those memories are locked in there with me. The day we walk out the door for the last time I expect it to hit hard, and I imagine I'll be subjected to a few hours of something akin to mourning when it's all finished.

But there's a flip side to all of that.

I'm hopelessly sentimental, and the stronger my memories of a place, the harder it is to let it go. The flip side, though, is the most valuable thing I've learned from having children (so far), and that flip side is this: there are always more memories to make. True, I can't toss Logan into the air the way I used to because he's too damn big (he might can toss me up in a few years, though!). I can't feed Abby a bottle and let her fall asleep on me anymore. I can't roughhouse with Logan because he isn't too far away from being able to kick my ass.

I can, though, play a game of H.O.R.S.E. with Logan now, and soon we'll be able to go one on one in basketball. I couldn't even pretend to do that two years ago. I plan to learn how to braid Abby's hair (I'm a manly man), since it's long enough for that now. I know there are books to read to her and movies to watch with both of them and board games to play. When they get older it'll get harder, sure, but there will always be memories to be made. What I've learned is that though it's harder than ever to let the past go, I know there's a future to look forward to. That's one of the things I've needed to learn for some time now, and all it took were the failures and nut shots and embarrassing moments in this book to make it happen.

So, if you're a new dad, get ready for the ride of your life. It's hard, but the hard parts pass. The amazing, life-changing parts are worth the hard parts multiplied times a hundred. If you're an older dad, kick back and relax in your sandals and socks, and know that you're probably more of a hero than you ever believed. Keep being that hero.

And snap buttons suck.

-Luke Whaley

ABOUT THE AUTHOR

Luke Whaley is a father of two who likes to write in the spare time he doesn't have. This is his first published work, mostly compiled from his online blog "How Not to Dad," and he is working feverishly to complete his debut horror/mystery novel titled *The Reach*. He lives in Alabama with his wife, Nikki, his two kids Logan and Abby, and his dog Ripley. Discover more about Luke by visiting the following websites:

lukewhaleyauthor.com
www.facebook.com/lukewhaley.author
www.instagram.com/author_l_whaley/